the Relaxation *therapy manual*

Christine Heron

WINSLOW

Telford Road • Bicester
Oxon OX6 0TS • UK

Dedication

To Kathleen and Maurice Heron

First published in 1996 by
Winslow Press Limited, Telford Road, Bicester, Oxon OX6 0TS,
United Kingdom
www.winslow-press.co.uk
Reprinted 1997, 1998

002–2603/Printed in the United Kingdom/1010

British Library Cataloguing in Publication Data

Heron, Christine
   The relaxation therapy manual
   1. Relaxation 2. Mental healing
   I. Title
   615.8'51

ISBN 0 86388 159 9

Contents

About the Author

Christine Heron is a qualified social worker and yoga teacher with many years' experience teaching relaxation skills. She has worked with people with mental health problems, with disabled people and has been a social work lecturer. Christine currently works as a social services manager and undertakes private training in yoga, meditation, relaxation skills and spiritual development.

Acknowledgements

Thanks to Donna Perrigo and Ian Cannon for their help in compiling this manual. Also to all colleagues and clients over the years who have helped me to learn relaxation skills.

Introduction

Relaxation skills have been taught in a wide range of settings for many years. Most often they are to be found in mental health units such as psychiatric hospitals or day centres, but they are also used with a whole range of people, including children, physically disabled people, those with learning disabilities and older people. A wide variety of professionals may undertake the delivery of these skills. Social workers, psychiatrists, nurses, occupational therapists and care workers may all be involved. Of these, many will have had little or no training in teaching relaxation.

The Relaxation Therapy Manual is a complete guide which enables people who already have basic skills in therapeutic work with clients to use relaxation techniques with both individuals and groups. It can be used by people who have no background in relaxation and also by those who are already experienced and who wish to refine their techniques. The manual is divided into four parts:

Part 1 gives the background information which forms a basis for relaxation techniques. This includes models which explain stress, tension and relaxation and ways to assess people's suitability for relaxation therapy. Ways of developing yourself as a therapist are examined, as is the creation of an environment which enhances the relaxation process.

In **Part 2** we look at a variety of relaxation techniques aimed at both mind and body. Ways in which these techniques can be creatively combined, and customized to suit the individual, are suggested.

Part 3 examines the application of relaxation therapy. There are a number of common problems which most trainers will come across, and ways of dealing with these are discussed. Relaxation can be undertaken with a range of client groups, and Section 12 shows how it can be best adapted to suit particular needs.

Finally, **Part 4** contains an eight-week relaxation course which provides a week-by-week guide to teaching people the relaxation skills discussed earlier in the manual. The course is made up of session plans, handouts to be photocopied and exercises.

Teaching people to relax can be a very rewarding experience. While some people will struggle to find the discipline to use the techniques, it is not uncommon to find others whose lives are transformed by learning these simple skills. Perhaps most importantly, the more relaxation you teach, the more relaxed you will become yourself!

Preparing for Relaxation Training 1

1 Background to Relaxation

Introduction

This section discusses the relationship between relaxation, tension and stress and explains what happens in our bodies when we are tense and when we are relaxed. This information can be useful for people who are learning to relax, since they will be better able to understand the processes that are going on in their bodies.

• • • Relaxation, Tension and Stress

There is now general agreement on a model which explains tension and relaxation: the well known 'fight or flight' mechanism. When a person faces threat or danger their sympathetic nervous system takes action to allow them to deal with the situation more effectively. Here are just some of the physiological changes which can occur:

- release of adrenalin, noradrenalin and cortisol into the bloodstream (stimulates reflexes and raises blood sugar for more energy);
- heart rate increases, blood vessels dilate and blood pressure rises (more blood is pumped to the lungs and muscles for action);
- breathing is faster and more shallow, air passages in the lungs dilate to enable more absorption of oxygen;
- energy is diverted to systems which need it, therefore areas such as the digestive and eliminatory systems slow down.

When the person has dealt with the danger — by fighting or running away — the parasympathetic nervous system goes into action, reversing the above and allowing the body to return to a state of rest.

This is a natural process and in primitive conditions is essential for the individual's survival. However, because of our increasingly complicated lives, 'civilized' humans become aroused by symbolic events rather than by actual physical threat. Take the person sitting in a traffic jam drumming their fingers on the steering wheel. They can become so frustrated that their sympathetic nervous system is engaged. Moreover·there is no action that can be taken in these circumstances: physically attacking the traffic lights is both futile and frowned upon! Therefore that person may not deactivate their arousal. They arrive at work in a state of simmering resentment and carry this throughout the day. In fact it is believed that many people are almost permanently in a state of 'fight or flight' arousal. Often unknown to themselves, they are experiencing physical tension and can be described as being in a state of stress.

• • • Interaction of Body, Mind and Emotions

In most cases tension does not just manifest itself at the physical level — it also gets translated into mental and emotional problems. Table 1 shows some of the conditions which indicate that a person is experiencing stress.

Table I Indicators of stress

Physical	Mental	Emotional
Headaches	Worry	Anger and irritability
Breathing problems	Frustration	Depression
Muscle and joint tension	Things out of proportion	Anxiety
Dizziness	Feeling burdened	Fear
Stomach upsets	Forgetful	Hopelessness
Sleep problems	Cannot concentrate	Feeling inadequate
Lack of energy	Difficulty making decisions	Being withdrawn
Feeling restless	Compulsions	Rapid mood changes
Feeling of irregular heartbeat	Extreme perfectionism	Feeling guilty
	Taking things personally	Persistent relationship problems
	Persistent negative thoughts	

These three levels all interact and reinforce each other, so that the whole personality is transformed. This can lead to what is known as 'burn out', a lack of interest and enthusiasm in life. In extreme cases it can result in severe depression, anxiety states, phobias and suicide.

For some people stress can develop into a physical illness. It has been suggested that the following conditions may be effected by stress: angina, high blood pressure, stomach disorders such as diverticulitis, cancer, migraine, asthma and skin complaints.

• • • How Relaxation Works

The basis of relaxation techniques is that they encourage the activation of what Benson (1975) called the 'Relaxation Response': the state of relaxation which occurs when an individual is at rest. However the important factor about 'fight or flight' de-arousal is that this is an *autonomic* reaction, one that is not under the individual's conscious control. Apart from adepts of yoga, few people are able to decrease their heartbeat at will.

Therefore relaxation techniques use systems which we can control, to affect those we cannot. For instance, in progressive relaxation we teach our muscles to relax, which then has an effect on the subtler systems of the body; with guided visualizations we present the mind with situations which are completely peaceful, thereby encouraging total deactivation.

Relaxation is a skill, not a mystery. Our bodies have become habitually used to high levels of tension, but we can reprogramme them with relaxation until this becomes our natural way of being. Deep relaxation also goes further than just resting the body. It has been found that a particular brain wave pattern, alpha waves, can be present when people are relaxing or meditating. These patterns are associated with subjective feelings of well-being and happiness. By relaxing we can alter our moods and outlook, and thereby effect great changes in our lives.

• • • The Use of Relaxation as Therapy

Relaxation techniques are generally used in one of the three following ways:

1 *To help people learn general, overall relaxation* This can be done for individuals or in groups.

2 *For use with specific problem areas* For instance, someone may have problems with physical tension in the stomach area which causes digestive problems, or a person may feel anxiety when shopping. Relaxation can also be used as part of an overall programme of therapeutic intervention for people who have specific anxiety problems or phobias.

3 *As part of another therapeutic approach* Relaxation can be incorporated into other therapies at appropriate stages,

particularly if there is a need to help the person achieve a relaxed and receptive state. An example of this would be in counselling for sexual abuse. If the person wishes to look at accepting the past, it may be helpful to get them to relax in order to open themselves to new ideas. Alternatively, in a cognitive therapy, a person might be encouraged to relax so they are receptive to positive statements to help them change their attitude to life.

The approach to relaxation in this manual is suitable for all the above purposes.

2 Assessment

Introduction

When people are referred for relaxation sessions it is advisable to assess whether relaxation is appropriate for them at this time or if other interventions would be helpful. This chapter outlines the factors which could be taken into account when making an assessment.

• • • Who can Benefit from Relaxation?

Relaxation is beneficial to people with a wide range of needs. Most obviously it is used with people suffering from stress and tension. This can range from someone who is in demanding employment and needs relaxation as a coping skill, to those whose lives are devastated by extreme anxiety and panic. Relaxation can improve quality of life, and for some people it can be a life-line.

Relaxation has health benefits other than those sought initially. Benson (1975) showed that some forms of relaxation will reduce respiratory rate, heart rate and oxygen consumption and can reduce high blood pressure. Therefore relaxation is used with a range of physical illnesses such as heart conditions, cancer and migraine, and as a means of controlling pain. In terms of medical conditions, the exercises described in this book are all extremely safe and gentle and, provided they are done in a non-forceful way, will be suitable for all physical conditions.

Both adults and children can successfully learn relaxation skills, while people with severe learning disabilities or dementia can be encouraged to relax by making the environment around them peaceful and relaxing. Indeed, since most of us suffer some form of stress, everyone can benefit from relaxation!

• • • Can Relaxation Stand Alone?

Relaxation is an extremely useful intervention, and for some people it will be the only change they need to make in order to feel happy with their lives. However, among some professionals, there has been the danger of relaxation being seen as a panacea, with relaxation sessions being prescribed for people with the unrealistic expectation that they will 'cure' their life problems.

Relaxation works by enabling people to remain physically relaxed and mentally detached in stressful circumstances. Often, however, this is not enough: the stresses that surround them are just too much to cope with. Relaxation techniques are strengthened and enhanced if people also learn other skills to deal with stress. Therefore relaxation is often combined with other approaches, predominantly the following.

Stress Management

This gives individuals the chance to examine their own lives and find out what is contributing to the way they feel. Solutions would then be looked at in terms of time management, setting up support networks, planning, coping strategies, and the like.

Cognitive Therapies

These work on the basis that our thoughts control our lives. We tend to have a constant inner dialogue, mainly filled with negative thoughts, images and beliefs, of which we are unaware. In these therapies the person discovers the nature of their 'self talk' and reprogrammes him or herself with positive dialogue. Useful accounts of these approaches can be found in Powell, *The Mental Health Handbook* (1992).

Assertiveness Training

This is for people who need to learn skills in how they relate to other people. Assertiveness teaches awareness of our rights as individuals, our responsibilities to other people, and gives skills for dealing with situations which many people find difficult, such as handling criticism, saying no, expressing an opinion, and so on. For more information see Holland & Ward, *Assertiveness: A Practical Approach* (1990).

Psychotherapies and Counselling

People who are depressed, confused or emotionally troubled may benefit from exploring their lives in much more depth, especially examining and trying to come to terms with events from the past which may have caused their current unhappiness.

• • • When is Relaxation Unsuitable?

Relaxation is not a *crisis intervention*. If someone has suffered a traumatic loss or any upsetting and disorienting set of circumstances, there is little point in sitting them down and getting them to visualize a beautiful garden — unless, that is, the person already has relaxation skills which can be called into play. As a rule, relaxation will come later in the healing process, when the person has started to work through the immediate emotional trauma.

People who are very *distressed* will not generally benefit from relaxation. Sandra had come to an initial interview for a relaxation group. She sat, tense as a board, wringing her hands together, answering my questions in monosyllables. Then my colleague asked gently, "Do you feel you deserve to relax?" This opened the floodgates. Sandra had recently had an abortion and was consumed with guilt about what she had done. At the end of the meeting we were able to suggest counselling, rather than relaxation, as an initial intervention. Privately we marvelled at a psychiatrist who could have thought she was in any condition to benefit from relaxation. Basically, people who are actively emotionally upset need to discharge that distress before thinking about relaxing.

Opinion varies as to whether people who feel *depressed* should undertake relaxation. The theory against this is that relaxation will send them further into themselves, whereas they need to be pulled out and energized. My personal feeling is that most depressed people are also anxious and it is difficult to separate the two. I would tend to leave the choice of whether or not to join the session to the individual. They could then decide whether they felt it was benefiting them or not.

It is usually futile to attempt the forms of relaxation described in this book with people who are so *agitated* they find it difficult to stay still. In a class they may need to wriggle or wander in and out, and therefore will be disruptive to others. In these situations the more active forms of relaxation can be tried: for instance massage, yoga, or even more dynamic forms of exercise, such as swimming.

It is often recommended that people who are diagnosed as having serious mental health problems such as those *labelled schizophrenic* should not undertake relaxation. I have found that, provided such individuals are not currently experiencing a disturbed period, many do in fact benefit from relaxation.

Finally a number of people are encouraged, or even forced, to undertake relaxation by other people, when they personally are unwilling. Connie's husband Arthur had multiple sclerosis and was becoming increasingly frustrated as his mobility decreased. Connie had dragged Arthur along to hear about relaxation, and the more she enthused the more he looked unimpressed. Eventually he agreed to try a few sessions, but dropped out after two weeks, saying it was a waste of time. Which it was — for Arthur — but not for Connie, who took over his slot, benefited enormously and went on to a regular yoga class. Usually, if someone is obviously unwilling and not interested, it is best to enable them to say no.

Table 2 Assessment for relaxation: summary

Positive Indicators for Relaxation	Negative Indicators for Relaxation	Referral for Further Therapy
Motivated and interested	Unwilling or forced	Needs to take charge of life events and understand stress: *Stress Management*
Anxious, stressed, tense	Person in crisis	
Stress condition such as phobia or panic attacks	Intense distress	Needs to combat negative self-talk: *Cognitive therapy or self-esteem building*
	Very agitated	
	Mentally disturbed	Unresolved emotional issues: *Counselling*
		Needs to manage anger or passivity: *Assertiveness, anger work*

3 Delivering a Relaxation Session

Introduction

The delivery of a relaxation session is all-important, making the difference between whether or not the group is able to relax. In this chapter we look at ways in which trainers can develop and improve their relaxation techniques.

• • • Manner: Relaxed, Calm and Confident

Relaxation trainers need, more or less, to embody the principles they are advocating for others. If you do not normally come across as a relaxed person, it will be necessary to develop a relaxed attitude, at least during the times you have contact with clients! The benefits from this, for you, are that by consciously doing this it is likely that you will become genuinely more relaxed.

Ideally the trainer will have a calm and confident manner. Calmness is important because it sets the client at ease and engenders a relaxed atmosphere from the moment of their meeting you. Remember that relaxation does not just begin when you start to talk someone down, but from the very moment that you meet each other for your session. Confidence is necessary because the client, especially at the beginning, may be feeling extremely anxious. After all, it is a great exercise of trust to go into a room with strangers and lie on the floor with your eyes closed!

Another reason for reflecting the state you want to encourage in the person is that they are likely to take their cue from you, unconsciously influenced by the atmosphere you create. First impressions are important. Perhaps there are manic and frenetic relaxation trainers, but I have never met one.

• • • Body Language

Body language should again reflect the nature of the relaxation session. Posture should be open — arms and legs uncrossed. Particular attention should be paid to the areas of the body which reveal hidden tension; the shoulders, for instance, should be down and back. If you are a tapper, twitcher, doodler or wriggler, leave these tendencies outside the session. So far as possible your body needs to be still. It can be useful to do a relaxation body scan on yourself: an experienced relaxation trainer thought that his body language was totally relaxed: it was only when, one summer, he wore open-toed sandals that he realized that his right big toe twitched almost constantly.

Breathing is, of course, intrinsic to body language. It is extremely important that the trainer's breathing should be relaxed. It has been shown that two people in proximity to each other will often start to breathe in a similar pattern. Thus, in the intimate and receptive environment of a relaxation session, the client will usually unconsciously imitate the breathing of the trainer.

During the session it is important to adopt a comfortable position which means you will not have to move around too much, thereby distracting the client. Of course everyone adopts their own individual style. A few people, for instance, prefer to stand when doing relaxation, some even prefer to walk around the room. The key point is that, whatever technique is adopted, it must not interfere with the client's concentration. If you do feel most comfortable walking, then it is important to move quietly and rhythmically, keeping a distance from the client. Sudden movements and noises are disturbing, while going too close to someone's personal space will make most people instinctively tense up.

The most usual position for the trainer is in a comfortable chair a few feet away from the person. One note of caution: it is useful not to get too comfortable. It is certainly not unknown for a trainer to get so relaxed they wake up with a horrible jerk, not knowing where they were in the relaxation, or even who they were with! If you know you tend to drift off during relaxation, you may need to sit on a hard chair, or even stand.

Finally, if relaxation is done on the floor, it is better, if possible, not to be positioned too high above the relaxers. Having someone looking down on them can make many people feel uneasy. In this case it is better, if you are able, to take the session sitting on the floor.

• • • Voice

Some of us are lucky enough to be blessed with the melodious and velvety tones which guarantee instant success as a relaxation trainer. For instance, I expect we can all think of school-teachers who manage to induce oblivion in a whole class with their, in the circumstances unfortunate, soothing tones. Most of us, however, have to work to improve on what nature has given us in the area of voice, and learn how to make an effective delivery.

While everyone develops their own individual style, there are a number of principles which are more or less constant.

Voice: Slow, Soft and Smooth

The most important point is that the voice should enhance relaxation, rather than distracting the individual. In relaxation we are attempting to quiet the individual's everyday consciousness and to make contact with the unconscious mind. To lull the ever-vigilant consciousness we need to speak softly and slowly. Smooth and easy delivery will have a further relaxing effect.

The rationale behind this is that the human body responds to certain signals. The soft, slow, smooth voice indicates that there is no danger and that it is safe to relax. High, fast, disjointed tones mean that the individual becomes alert, mind and body ready to react to any stimulus. This whole process is similar to what happens when we are trying to get babies to sleep. Basically we play lullabies, not the '1812 Overture'. If these principles are observed, the individual has the basics for delivering a good relaxation session.

Pattern: Rhythm, Repetition and Pause

As the trainer becomes more experienced they can experiment with a number of techniques. *Rhythm* usually involves accentuating particular words or syllables so that the phrases used take on a particular pattern. For instance:

you are relaxing your left leg completely

becomes

Yooou are relaxing your left leg completely

Again a rhythmical delivery will lull the conscious mind, which comes to anticipate the emphases in tone. Rhythms can be subtly altered to obtain particular effects in relaxation. Slowing down will deepen the effects, while quickening will start to alert people.

Repetition is intrinsic to all forms of relaxation. Repeating significant words, phrases and rhythms is used extensively in hypnosis and has the effect of switching off the conscious mind and activating the unconscious. In relaxation it can be used to repeat instructions, and emphasize particular states:

You feel you are floating... floating... floating on a cloud. You feel so light and relaxed, light and relaxed.

Pauses have a number of important uses in relaxation. They are a means by which the person relaxing can assimilate the information they are receiving. A constant flow of commentary gives too much information and does not allow the unconscious mind to absorb what is happening. Pauses deepen relaxation because they give a sense of space and timelessness to the process. They can also give people an 'active' role, time in which to take control of their relaxation.

Pauses can be of varying length and can take place throughout the relaxation session. They can last from a couple of seconds to a pause at the end of a session which may last five to ten minutes. After a medium-to-long pause be careful that the first word you speak is especially soft to allow the relaxers to readjust. Generally the length of any pause at the end of the session will depend on the background of the relaxers. The more experienced they are, the longer they can lie in silence. The trainer needs to be aware that silences, with nothing to do, can make some people feel anxious.

Other Styles

There are innumerable other relaxation styles which can be adopted. Some people develop a melodious, 'sing-song' delivery, while others prefer a monotone. Some trainers are very expressive, putting feeling into words. 'Breathe', for instance, may be said in such a way that it comes out with a sigh. All these can be very effective, but it is important that they should feel natural to you, not forced.

Delivering relaxation sessions is fun and creative. The main message must be to develop your own particular style and to 'tune in' to what works for individuals or groups.

• • • **Common Faults in Relaxation Delivery**

The most common faults are:

- going too fast,
- not pausing,
- gabbling,
- going too slow,
- voice too soft, so that people cannot hear you,
- reading word-for-word from a paper,
- idiosyncrasies which you may not be aware of: for instance, saying "OK" constantly, or grinding your teeth.

In relation to reading word-for-word, it is certainly acceptable for people who are new to relaxation to have brief notes on what they are going to cover in the session. I have, however, seen extensive notes used, to the extent where a trainer will read solidly through three closely written pages of 'Now stretch and relax your right big toe. Now stretch and relax your left big toe', which must have been a feat of endurance for all concerned. If you are reading word-for-word the client will know it. They will not relax as easily and will, quite rightly, lose confidence in you.

Personal idiosyncrasies are a more difficult area. These may be off-putting to some people, but not to others. I once attended a class where the teacher rolled all her 'rs' like an extra from 'Allo, Allo' and I became increasingly tense as I waited for the next 'r' word to be tortured. After the session I was surprised to find that most people were praising the teacher highly.

Another issue to be aware of is that some people adopt 'special relaxation voices' which can sound false. Also strong regional accents may be off-putting, especially if you are relaxing people who do not come from your area.

• • • Practice and Evaluation

In order to make sure you deliver your relaxation session in the most effective manner it is useful both to practise and to evaluate yourself. Practice is vital if you are new to relaxation. Talk through your sessions on your own until you feel confident with your style and your ability to find the right words.

Evaluation is useful for both new and experienced relaxation trainers. There are a number of useful ways of doing this. Carrying out relaxation sessions with friends or colleagues who are able to give informed feedback is extrememly effective. Tape-recordings of your session and, if you can bear it, video work, are also helpful. Watching or listening to recordings of yourself will invariably reveal areas on which you need to work.

Another method is, of course, asking for feedback from the participants in your sessions. Formal feedback is useful at the end of any course. However people are not always willing to give constructive criticism because they may see you in a position of power or may not want to hurt your feelings. Unsolicited informal feedback is a very good guide, as is observing people at the end of your session. There should be a peaceful, contemplative feeling after relaxation. People may be reluctant to get up from their mat or seat. If they are rushing to their feet or cannot wait to get out of the room, then, unless they have obvious anxiety problems, you may need to look at the effectiveness of your session. Similarly many people will spontaneously say how effective they found the relaxation. Comments such as "I didn't want to get up", "I didn't want to come back" or "I could have stayed there much longer" are frequent, and show that you are on the right lines.

4 Creating a Relaxing Environment

Introduction

Creating the right environment is very important for success in relaxation. Some environmental factors such as quietness and warmth are essential, while others serve to enhance the experience. Relaxation rooms vary from the simple to the elaborate and from cheap to costly. In this chapter we consider a number of suggestions for establishing and improving relaxation space. Examples of stockists of equipment mentioned in this chapter are listed at the end of the manual.

• • • Essentials for Relaxation

Quiet, Warmth and Comfort

Without these conditions it will be practically impossible to establish relaxation. *Quiet* means free from continual background noises, sudden disturbing noise and interruptions. This can be extremely difficult to achieve in its purest form. Noise from corridors or traffic outside are all difficult to control. So far as possible, have your room away from roads and areas inside your building which might be noisy. See Section 11 for solutions to this problem.

Warmth is essential because, if a person is cold, they will be thinking about this discomfort rather than relaxing. If you cannot achieve a suitable level of warmth with heating alone, people can use blankets and sleeping bags. These may be useful even in a warm room, since lying still for half an hour will lower the body temperature. If a room is very draughty it may prove impossible to relax lying on the floor, and chairs will have to be used.

Comfort is necessary for the same reasons as warmth. People need a mat to lie on which is sufficiently firm to support them, but soft enough not to cause discomfort. Rubber exercise or yoga mats are ideal, preferably placed on a carpeted floor. Chairs again need to be suitable. For relaxation the ideal type of chair gives the back support up to and including the head. Good-quality armchairs and recliners are suitable. A cheaper compromise is reclining sun loungers which are comfortable and give support and also a cheerful Mediterranean quality to a room!

NB The relaxation room must be a non-smoking environment.

••• Enhancing the Environment

A Special Room

If at all possible, it is useful to have a room which is set aside solely for relaxation. There are a number of reasons for this: the atmosphere created by successive sessions takes hold of the room, giving it a still and peaceful quality; sometimes rooms can be so relaxing that people can be affected just by going through the door. Conversely, if a room is used for other activities, these will leave their mark on the atmosphere. Many therapy rooms 'double up' for relaxation, which can cause problems since, if the person's last experience there was of crying in a counselling session, they are likely to associate this with the room. For practical convenience a set room means you do not have to spend time at the start and end of every session rearranging it.

However, owing to demands on space, it is often impossible to have a room solely for relaxation purposes. In this case it is helpful to prepare the room before people enter it: that is, close the curtains, light an aromatherapy oil burner, put on music — all of which can transform a room.

Decorations and Furnishings

Ideally the room will be carpeted, with heavy curtains which can keep out the light. Ornaments should enhance the uplifting, relaxing feel to the room. Ideal are plants, dried or fresh flowers and crystals. Paintings or pictures should perferably be of natural scenes or abstract in nature, rather than of people, which can promote associations.

Colour

Colour is extremely important in your room, since some colours are more suitable for relaxation than others (see Table 3). Generally colours used should be pastel or clear, not murky or gaudy. Dark colours, such as brown, black or deep blue, are not suitable, and bright colours such as red are energizing rather than relaxing.

Finally the walls in some relaxation rooms are white. This is often because projectors are used which create the best effects on white walls. (See Snoezelen, below.) White is

Table 3 Colours suitable for relaxation rooms and guided visualizations

Blues	A peaceful energy Soft and relaxing
Pinks	Warm and inviting Rose pink symbolizes love and creative intuition A feeling of safety and calm
Greens	Harmony and sympathy Associated with energy and growth
Yellows	The colour of the mind and intellect Uplifting and energizing Gold is the colour of high spirituality
Lilacs/mauve	Relaxing and especially good for meditation

a suitable colour for relaxation, but some people feel it can be too stark, and reminiscent of an institution.

Colours can be used in many imaginative combinations to make the room as attractive as possible. For instance, ceilings can be painted blue with white clouds, or with gold stars. Murals can be painted on the walls; country scenes, sunsets, waterfalls and so on are all suitable.

Music

Most relaxation rooms have music centres. Ideally speakers will be spaced around the room so that people get an equal share of the volume. If portable systems are used, care must be taken that the people closest to them do not get blasted while those in the far corners are straining to hear.

The purpose of music in relaxation is to create the right mood and enhance the experience. Care should be taken not to use it all the time so that the individual comes to rely on it to relax. Suitable music is soft, calming and repetitive. There is now a great deal of music which is specially composed for the purposes of relaxation. This might include pan-pipes, strings, pianos, choirs and also natural sounds such as flowing water, the wind or bird song. For variety's sake it is useful to have a number of different tapes, some for general relaxation, others to co-ordinate with a guided visualization. For instance, a country morning tape could be played as you take people on a visualized walk through the countryside.

Many different forms of music are suitable for relaxation, so long as they conform to the above principles. Music creates a special form of vibration, so care should be taken to make sure it feels harmonious. Certain forms of classical music may actually be discordant or depressing. It is best to avoid instrumental versions of well known songs, since these may have non-relaxing associations for people.

Equipment

Equipment should include relaxation mats, comfortable chairs and straight-backed chairs for meditation. Foam blocks (30 × 20 × 5 cm) can be useful for putting under the head, for sitting on to support the spine in meditation, and for supporting other parts of the body as necessary. Similarly useful are cushions and bolsters of varying size.

Fragrance

Fragrance is an extremely useful method of enhancing relaxation and creating a suitable atmosphere in the room. Women in particular appreciate a scented room; men sometimes find the smells off-putting. By far the best method of scenting a room is to use aromatherapy oils. In contrast to synthetic fragrances, pure essential oils have healing properties which can have subtle effects on people's moods.

The following oils are particularly suitable for promoting relaxation and reducing tension, depression, anxiety and insomnia: lavender, sandalwood, patchouli, geranium, camomile, juniper, ylang-ylang, rose, neroli and jasmine. The last three oils are extremely expensive and, for the purposes of scenting a room, are best bought already diluted.

There are a number of different methods for diffusing aromatherapy scents. Oil burners are now available in a variety of shops. Mix five drops each of up to three different oils to create a beautiful aroma. Also available are plug-in electric diffusers, and terra-cotta rings to put on lamps. If there is no specialist equipment available, oil could occasionally be dropped on the carpet.

Lighting

While the room should be predominantly dark, total blackness can be off-putting to participants and impractical for the trainer who needs to observe the group. Lighting should be subdued, and preferably not overhead, as this might disturb anyone lying beneath it. Candles are one option, so long as care is taken over fire safety. Alternatively table lamps can be used.

Water

While water is undeniably relaxing, it is also expensive. In terms of affordable items, the fish tank is always popular, especially with children. Also available are ornamental waterfalls, obtainable from some craft shops, in which water gently cascades over pebbles.

If money is no object there are a number of specialist items for watery relaxation. Jacuzzi-type pools and flotation tanks, darkened tanks in which people lie suspended in salt water, can all be used. These are especially effective for people with special needs, and those who find it hard to relax in other ways. However these items are all extremely expensive and specialized, involving time and upkeep. Water pools, for instance, need to be checked daily for temperature and chemical component to make sure they are safe to use. I have also come across a relaxation room which houses a noisy, chlorine-smelling, plastic jacuzzi, stuck in the corner as if it had just escaped from the municipal baths. Such large watery equipment has no place in a relaxation room.

Snoezelen★

Snoezelens are specialist areas composed of a number of items which stimulate the senses. They started in Holland and are predominantly used for people with learning disabilities, autistic people and people with sensory disabilities who respond to simple stimuli. They are also suitable for children and people with dementia, and can be enjoyed by anyone.

Items in a Snoezelen may include large foam mattresses and padded shapes, water and air beds, ball pools (containers filled with plastic balls, which mould themselves to the person's shape), lighting such as spotlights, projectors, ultraviolet lights, mirror balls, bubble tubes, vibrating walls and floors, music, electronic sounds, musical instruments, fragrances and items to taste.

Basically the Snoezelen is a place where people can explore, using all the senses. It is therefore a stimulating environment. However the general effect is also relaxing and it is said that people tend to relax within 10 to 15

★SNOEZELEN is a registered trademark. See 'Stocklists of Equipment' in the Appendix for details of where to obtain further information about SNOEZELEN in the UK and the USA.

minutes of entering the room. This experience therefore enables people who would not be able to understand the principles of relaxation to experience its effects.

Biofeedback Machines

Biofeedback machines monitor tension in the body and feed this back to the client in terms of particular sounds. By controlling the sound the individual learns to consciously control the autonomic nervous system. Biofeedback is an effective method of teaching people to relax and was widely used in the 1970s and 1980s, although currently it appears to have gone out of fashion.

Relaxation Techniques

2

5 General Principles for All Relaxation Techniques

Introduction

While relaxation techniques vary in style and emphasis, there are a number of points which are common to all. The following factors should be taken into account in preparation for your session:

1 People should go to the lavatory before relaxation.
2 Shoes should be taken off, and any tight clothing loosened, especially at the waist and neck.
3 Relaxation should not be done directly after a meal — the digestive system will slow down and not do its job correctly — nor before bedtime, as it will become associated with sleep. If you want to use a technique as a help against insomnia, choose one which is specific to this purpose.
4 Relaxation is *never* forcing, straining or willing; relaxation is *always* releasing, letting go, allowing.

It is very important that the relaxation should be practised regularly. It is only by constant use that we can truly learn the skills involved. Once the principles of relaxation are truly assimilated, then the practice can be less regular. The length of sessions may range from 20 minutes to an hour; 30 minutes is probably the optimal length of time.

The aim of relaxation is to remain conscious, not to go to sleep. The alpha brainwave pattern is not usually found in sleep, which indicates that relaxation and sleep are different experiences. It is said that 20 minutes' true relaxation is so refreshing that it reduces the need for sleep. If people habitually fall asleep in the session they need to look at the timing of it, and whether there is any reason they are so tired. It may be helpful to relax in a chair for a while to break the pattern.

There is a beginning, middle and end to relaxation sessions. The beginning involves introducing the idea of relaxation, and the middle deepening the experience. The end of relaxation is particularly important. People need to be 'brought back' into the room where they are: relaxation can be disorienting and it is useful to give them time to focus before going out of the class, especially before driving. Examples of focusing include general chat or physical activity, such as putting the mats away. Warning should be given that the light is about to be put on: people need the chance to cover their eyes until they adjust. People lying on the floor need to be able to stretch and roll over onto their side before getting up.

Trainers should only use touch, that is massage, in relaxation, in accordance with the procedures of their organization.

6 Postures for Relaxation

Introduction

Physical posture has a significant effect on people's ability to relax. This chapter will show the basic lying and sitting postures, and variations for people with special needs.

• • • Lying Postures

The most effective lying posture for all relaxation techniques is thousands of years old. 'Savasana', the yoga corpse posture, remains the classic relaxation position (see Table 4). This is because it is the position which allows the maximum possible relaxation for the body, which is in total alignment.

Table 4 Principles of the classical relaxation position

Body	Lying on the back in a straight line Body symmetrical to left and right
Legs	Apart to an angle of about 30 degrees Feet falling out to the side slightly
Pelvis	Tucked forward and upward, eliminating pressure on lower back
Back	As much in contact with floor as possible
Shoulder blades	Tucked under slightly, allowing the shoulders to sink down and the chest area to widen and open
Arms	Away from the body to an angle of up to 30 degrees Backs of hands on floor Shoulders rotated so the thumb side is closer to the ground than the little finger, opening the chest
Neck and head	Avoid compression in back of neck by elongating it, tucking the chin slightly in to the chest Head aligned symmetrically on the neck

Preliminary Exercises

In order to relieve any tension in the lower back, and to get as much contact between the back and the floor as possible, participants should bend their knees with their feet on the floor, then slowly release the legs away. This can be taken further by bringing the knees in to the chest. If the arms are clasped around the legs and the person rocks gently from side to side, the spine is massaged.

Surface

The surface for the classical pose should be comfortable but firm. A mat on a carpeted floor is ideal, as is a wide therapist's couch for those unable to get to the floor. Beds are not particularly suitable, since they are likely to be too soft, allowing the muscles to sag.

Alternatives to the Classical Pose

A number of people will not find the classical pose comfortable. This can be due to physical stiffness or disability, anxiety or habit. Two particular areas which often cause discomfort are the neck and the curve in the lower back: the lumbar spine (see Table 5).

Table 5 Remedial postures

Neck discomfort	Support the head with a yoga block or cushion, which lengthens the back of the neck and points the chin towards the chest
Lumbar spine discomfort	A cushion or bolster can be placed between the spine and the floor to support it
	The knees can be bent, with heels towards buttocks and feet flat on the floor. The head should be supported by a cushion, as for treating neck discomfort. Palms on lower abdomen (an Alexander Technique position)
	A surface can be built of blocks which supports the body from the head down to the lower back; the pelvis is on the floor; it should be sufficiently wide to support the shoulders; the head is usually supported as above
	The person can lie on their back with their knees bent and calves on the seat of a chair at the appropriate height for them

Must it be on the Back?

Some people are uncomfortable in the classical pose and say they cannot relax on their backs: when they go to sleep at night they always sleep on their sides or stomachs. The simple answer to this is, of course, that they are not supposed to be going to sleep! In fact it is better to have a position which is not associated with sleep, since it guards against any tendency to nod off. The reasons people dislike the posture may be its strangeness, because they are not used to lying on their back and habitually lie in some other way, or the anxiety it causes: this is, after all, a very vulnerable position. In physiological terms, the stomach area, which can easily sustain life-threatening injuries, is unprotected and open to attack, while the genital area is also vulnerable.

If at all possible, it is better if people try to persevere with the posture, since alternatives such as lying on the side do not allow all the muscles to relax. If people really do not like the classic posture or variations, the best alternative is to sit in a chair.

One final point: it is important to recognize if someone has deep anxiety connected with a particular position. In one of my classes there was a woman who was just not able to allow her legs to open to either side. I would go round and correct her posture and the minute I moved on her legs were back together, like a pair of scissors. I recognized there was some issue involved here, and left her to lie in the way of her choice. At the end of one class she told me that she had been sexually abused, and lying with her legs open felt too threatening.

• • • Sitting Postures

While sitting postures do not allow such a complete physical relaxation as the supine poses, they are sometimes necessary — if the person is not able to lie comfortably or the room is not appropriate for lying down. At the same time, sitting postures are very good for techniques which focus on mental relaxation. Indeed sitting is the preferred posture for meditation.

Sitting postures for relaxation (see Table 6) should follow the principles of supine relaxation positions. They

Table 6 Principles of sitting for relaxation and meditation

Body	Symmetrical and aligned throughout
Spine	Supported by the chair; use cushions if necessary Erect and stretching up
Feet and legs	Legs slightly parted, side by side, not crossed Feet full on the floor; use blocks or phone books if they will not reach
Shoulder blades	Down and in to allow the shoulders to sink down and the chest to open
Chest	Breast bone slightly raised so chest does not sink in, inhibiting breathing
Arms and hands	Arms by the sides, hands in the lap, palms up
Neck and head	Back of neck elongated Chin tucked in slightly Top of head pointing to the ceiling

should not be anything like the way that most of us sit. Gone will be the slump, the twist and the sprawl! Here the correct equipment is vital. Chairs should be firm and supporting, especially at the lumbar spine and neck.

Postures for Meditation

In meditation it is extremely important that the spine should be erect. People who wish to undertake meditation regularly could work on their back muscles so as to be able to support the spine without the chair back.

While we may have fond images of sitting down on the floor to meditate, for many people this is just not possible. Meditating in a chair is just as useful as the traditional cross-legged positions. Indeed, unless I was working with yoga students who were used to sitting on the floor, I would tend to use a chair to teach meditation in the initial stages. However, for those that wish to practise sitting in classical poses, there are two main positions.

Sitting positions can go from the simple crossed legs that we learn at school, to the full lotus, each foot supported on the opposite thigh (*only for the very supple*). In either case a block placed under the two sitting bones makes it easier to keep the spine erect. In a *kneeling* position the individual kneels on either side of a supported surface — meditation stool or a stack of blocks — which is of the correct height, usually four to six inches (10 - 14cm), to avoid knee strain and support the spine.

7 Progressive Relaxation

Introduction

Progressive relaxation (PR) is the most widely used relaxation technique. It often forms the basis of relaxation sessions prior to the use of more creative methods such as visualization. This chapter gives all the information needed to teach basic PR and some suggestions for more advanced techniques.

• • • Background

Progressive relaxation was developed by an American doctor, Edmund Jacobson, in the early years of this century. It basically involves focusing on, then relaxing, muscles and muscle groups in the body. Thus it *progresses* from feet to head, with each part of the body successively relaxing until total relaxation is achieved.

As originally established, PR was an exhaustive and presumably exhausting process, in which people undergoing the therapy would have countless sessions, focusing minutely on muscles for weeks on end. Classical PR can still be practised in this way. However the intensive nature of the technique was not suitable for many therapeutic settings, and it was also found that similar relaxation effects could be achieved with less effort. Subsequently, then, it has been amended by practitioners to make it simpler and less time consuming. The approach to PR discussed in this chapter is one which I have found particularly effective.

• • • How Progressive Relaxation Works

PR is based on the principle that anxiety and deep muscle relaxation cannot co-exist. Therefore, if people learn how to relax their muscles, not only will they physically relax, but their anxiety will also be reduced. PR thus reflects the interplay between body and mind: relax the body and the mind will be calmed. It is also a method of using muscles that are under voluntary control to relax systems of the body that are autonomic.

The technique is especially useful for newcomers to relaxation, for a number of reasons.

Body Awareness

Many people become so accustomed to physical tension in their bodies that they literally do not know it is there. I recall one social work student, who could not lie still for more than five minutes and suffered from chronic insomnia, telling me that he thought he was a relaxed person. PR teaches people to recognize the difference between tension and relaxation in their bodies and gives them a choice on how they prefer to be.

Quick and Practical Benefits

PR is a skill which nearly everyone can learn quickly. Success is practically guaranteed from an early stage, because some degree of relaxation inevitably follows from consciously stretching muscles. This encourages people to stick with the technique and eventually go into deeper levels of relaxation. It is also easily understood and active in nature. People learning PR find their bodies and minds occupied. They are able to move and stretch. This is helpful for people who might get anxious if they felt compelled to lie still and relax.

Moreover, once learned, PR can be applied in a number of situations. Once tension awareness and release are accomplished, the person can, and should, utilize them throughout their lives, not just in the relaxation session. For instance, we can relax while driving the car, sitting in the office, out walking or standing in supermarket queues. People gain control over their muscles and thus feel more in control of their lives. This leads on to the skill of what Jacobson called 'differential relaxation'.

• • • Differential Relaxation

In our everyday lives there are a number of ways in which physical tension can impede our actions. One form involves putting far more effort into an action than is needed. This is quite common with motor movements of the hands — holding a pencil so tight that it breaks, or gripping the steering wheel until the knuckles go white. It also applies to other movements, for example stomping rather than walking, or chewing on sponge cake as if it was toffee. Alternatively more muscles are used than are necessary to do a task. A driver may find that, rather than just use the muscle groups needed to steer, indicate, change gear and so on, they have tensed from their shoulders to the top of their head. The person who has anxiety about using their computer may unknowingly be knotting their stomach into a ball while their fingers deftly travel the keyboard. Of course these two forms of tension often occur together and reinforce each other.

In differential relaxation, the skills learnt in PR are applied to specific muscle groups in everyday situations.

••• General Principles of Progressive Relaxation

A full PR induction is included as a handout in Session 2 of the Relaxation Course. PR is divided into four stages: attention, stretching, releasing tension and awareness of relaxation.

Attention

This involves the individual 'taking their awareness' to areas of the body. The aim is that they start to recognize the difference between tension and relaxation. Instructions include:

Be aware of...
Take your attention to...
Let your awareness flow into...

Stretching

Stretching is the second stage. It involves accentuating any tension felt in the area as a prelude to relaxation. Originally this stage of PR involved *tensing* the muscles. Modern theory, however, recommends stretching rather then tensing. The reason for this is that a gentle elongation of muscles produces immediate tension release — rather like stretching, then relaxing elastic — whereas constricting muscles carries the danger that they will maintain, rather than release, the tension. This becomes obvious when we think about how we naturally try to release tension. First thing in the morning we stretch our bodies, rather than curling them into a ball.

A variety of gentle but focused stretching exercises can be used. Often they involve moving the part in opposite directions: the foot, for instance, can be flexed to the ceiling and then pointed away from the body. This is so that the pairs of muscles which stretch and contract in turn to promote movement can both be relaxed. The stretches should be smooth rather than forced or jerky. Some people will be inclined to over-exert. Relaxation is to do with awareness and letting go, not teeth-gritting endurance which will actually promote more tension.

Stretches are usually held for three to six seconds. However people should be told that they are in charge of their own bodies and not to do any exercise they do not want to, or to hold for a second longer than they feel is comfortable.

Release

This is the stage in which a natural letting go of tension will occur. The trainer's job is to deepen and accentuate this release by highlighting the sensations experienced at this time. Suggestions will include images which focus on the feelings of release. Examples include:

Feel how the tension flows away from your muscles...

Your shoulders are letting go completely...

A wonderful, warm feeling of relaxation flows into your hands...

Your stomach is letting go...

Wave upon wave of relaxation is flowing into your body...

The heavy tension flows away. Your body is becoming lighter and lighter...

Key words are: *Warmth, flowing, relaxing, releasing, letting go, lightness, heaviness, waves, ripples, softening, melting, floating.*

Awareness of Relaxation

At this stage the individual learns to recognize the feeling of relaxation, with the aim of making this the body's natural state.

• • • Muscle Groups

The direction in Progressive Relaxation invariably goes up the body from toes to head, often in the following order: feet, legs, buttocks, pelvis, stomach, back and spine, shoulder blades, chest, hands, arms, shoulders, neck, face: jaw, mouth, cheeks, forehead, eyes, ears, scalp. Where there are two parts to the body, feet for example, these are often done right then left. If a person is left-handed, some trainers prefer to reverse the order.

••• Variations on Basic Technique

1 One approach is to focus on tiny areas of the body. For instance, instead of the foot we would cover individual toes, the ball of foot, the instep and so on. This can be useful with very tense people and in doing relaxation with individuals to discover tension areas.

2 A number of body areas are notorious for holding onto tension. While these vary between individuals they usually involve, individually or in combination, buttocks (anal region), stomach, shoulders, neck, jaw, mouth or forehead. It is often worth concentrating on these areas, suggesting that people pay particular attention to them when relaxing.

3 The inner organs and the skin are 'hidden' areas in the body which can benefit from relaxation. It is not practical to stretch these parts, so the technique will involve awareness, then release. In general people are pretty hazy about the geography of their bodies, so it can be helpful if the trainer gives some idea of where the inner organs are found. The skin can either be relaxed at the same time as the individual body parts it encloses, or as a separate entity after the parts have been covered. The latter is a particularly relaxing effect, as the whole body can be encouraged to soften.

••• Advanced Techniques

The aim of PR is that people should develop a high level of awareness and control of muscular tension. As people become more experienced they are able to take charge of their own relaxation, with less formal suggestion. The following are options which can be useful with more advanced groups.

Whole Body Stretch and Release

The arms are taken over the head and the body is elongated. This is often done three times at the start of a session which then focuses on mental relaxation.

Progressive Awareness and Release

The attention is taken up through the body and the parts are relaxed without physical stretching.

The Use of Imagery to Release Muscular Tension

Colour and
shape

The body is checked for tension. If any is found it is given a colour and a shape. This is then diffused into a cloud and floats away.

Balloons   Balloons are attached to parts of the body. The strings are cut and as they float away the tension goes with them.

Earth   Tension flows from the body into the earth below.

River of light   People imagine they are lying in a river of light. Tension flows away into the river.

8 Breathing

Introduction

The breath is intimately connected with relaxation. A popular remedy for anxiety states is to tell people to breathe deeply. Unfortunately most people do not have an understanding of how to breathe correctly. This chapter will examine the use of breathing techniques for relaxation.

• • • Respiration and Circulation

The purpose of respiration is to enable oxygen to be supplied to the body and for toxins to be released. Oxygen is passed from the lungs to the heart, where it is pumped through the body. Every three minutes it returns to the heart and the toxins which have been collected on the journey back are transmitted into the lungs, from where they are exhaled. Without a supply of oxygen and a discharge of toxins, cells — indeed the whole system — will die.

Together the respiratory and circulatory systems are powerful forces. They cause a rhythm in our bodies, the rhythm of the breath and of the heart beat. If we can encourage these two systems to function harmoniously together we are on our way to good health and boundless energy.

• • • Breathing Problems

Unfortunately, while we generally inhale sufficient oxygen to live, most of us are functioning at a much lower level than we need for good health. It is said that we learn bad breathing habits once we lose the natural ability of the young child. Bad posture, a sedentary lifestyle, constricting clothes and stress are the causes. The effects on the respiratory system include shallow chest breathing, panting breath, gasping breath, puffing out of the chest, swelling of the abdomen, raising of the shoulders, a rigid chest and forgetting to breathe altogether!

Links between stress and breathing problems are well documented. When an individual is under stress their breathing is likely to become shallow and fast as they try to absorb oxygen quickly. What actually happens is that insufficient oxygen is obtained, toxins are not released and there is wear and tear on the body. The effects on the individual resulting from this are wide and varied. On the mental level there can be fatigue, lack of concentration, irritability, sleep problems and depression. Physically people may experience lack of ability to renew body tissues, damage to skin, bones, teeth and hair, digestive problems, liver problems, respiratory problems (inactive lungs are a moist, warm, breeding ground for bacteria) and a general predisposition to illness and obesity.

• • • Breathing and Relaxation

The benefits of correct breathing reverse many of the above problems. Energy circulates through the body, which means that tissues regenerate, fatigue is reduced and concentration improves, as does the ability to sleep well. Similarly there is a greater equanimity of mood and resistance to illness through a general cleansing of the system.

There is an extremely close relationship between breathing and relaxation: if the breath is tense, the body cannot relax completely; if the breath is relaxed, the body will be encouraged to relax also. Therefore there are two aims for the use of breath in relaxation: to change bad breathing habits and learn correct breathing, and to relax the breath and use this to enhance relaxation in the body and mind. Because relaxed breathing is not natural to many people, it can be helpful to teach some simple breathing exercises, either before another form of relaxation or as a relaxation technique itself.

• • • General Principles of Relaxed Breathing

Slow, Deep, Even and Easy

Slow breathing gives time for oxygen to be absorbed by the body and for toxins to be collected. It is estimated that it takes 10 to 20 seconds for the optimum amount of oxygen to be made available for circulation. Eastern thought is that we do not have a set number of years in our lives, but a fixed number of breaths: if we breathe slowly we increase our life span! In view of the health benefits associated with correct breathing, there seems to be some evidence to support this idea.

Deep breathing is necessary for total inhalation and exhalation, using the whole of the lungs. *Even* breathing means that there are no jerks or pauses in the process. The breathing flows smoothly in and out, with a constant pattern. Most importantly the breath must never be forced: it should be *allowed* to flow in and out *easily*.

If all the above points are adopted, the individual will develop a smooth, rhythmic way of breathing which will replace their old respiratory habits.

Additional Points

The posture for relaxed breathing involves wide chest, relaxed shoulders, raised breast bone. Relaxed breathing practice can be done either lying or sitting. Breathing should always take place through the nose. The mucous membrane and hairs of the respiratory system serve to keep toxins, bacteria and foreign bodies from reaching the lungs. Also the air is warmed by travelling through the nasal passages before reaching the lungs. People who are unable to breathe through the nose may be advised to consult their doctor.

The breathing apparatus should consciously be relaxed. Attention should be given to the diaphragm, rib cage (all the way round), shoulders, lungs, respiratory tract, throat, mouth, nose and face muscles.

• • • Exercise: The Complete Breath

The complete breath enables people to breathe with the *whole of their lungs*, thus correcting many common breathing problems. The lungs are larger than many people think. They stretch from the diaphragm, a large muscle at the bottom of the rib cage, up to the top of the chest. Similarly they are not hollow balloons, but firm, sponge-like organs which are divided horizontally into lobes.

The complete breath is in three stages (see Table 7): first, people learn to activate the lower lungs by breathing into

Table 7 Instructions for complete breath

Low or diaphragmatic breathing	Attention is taken to the diaphragm. The ribs are encouraged to expand very slightly out and to the sides. Only the top part of the abdomen will rise. The stomach should not be puffed out. People can put their hands on their lower rib cage with fingertips just touching in the centre; when they breathe in the fingers will separate.
Mid- or intercostal breathing	Attention is taken to the mid-chest. The ribs are felt to expand slightly to the sides and under the armpits. The hands can be moved to the sides of the rib cage to increase awareness.
High or clavicluar breathing	Attention is taken to the upper chest. The sternum (breast bone) is allowed to rise slightly, without raising the shoulders. The hands can be placed just under the collar bone on either side.
Breathing out	Reverse the above instructions.

that area; next the mid-lungs and finally the upper chest area are activated. Once proficient in these stages, individuals undertake the complete breath which combines them into one smooth, continuous breath.

• • • Uses of Relaxed Breathing

In Everyday Life

The complete breath is extremely useful for relaxing in everyday situations. Relaxed breathing can help people who have tension in particular activities in the same way as differential relaxation. Often these two techniques can be combined for this purpose.

In Relaxation Sessions

In the course of a relaxation session the breath is likely to become more shallow. This is because the bodily systems are slowing down and less oxygen is needed. The out breath is of great importance in relaxation. It is through exhalation — letting go — of breath that the body relaxes most deeply. The whole *rhythm* of relaxed breathing sends waves of relaxation through the body. When breath is slow, smooth and even it has a hypnotic effect on the individual.

The trainer needs to stress that all breathing techniques must be done in a way which feels comfortable to the individual. There must be no straining. It is important to be aware that focusing on the breath can be uncomfortable for some people, and if this is the case it may be best to omit these techniques.

• • • Breathing Techniques

Breathing can be used in combination with other techniques, such as progressive relaxation, to enhance the experience by focusing attention at intervals on the breathing. Suggestions include the following:

Take your attention to your breathing

Your breathing is relaxing

On every in breath you breathe in relaxation; as you breathe out you let go completely

Your breath is flowing in and out, in and out. You relax more and more

Breathing can also be used as the basis for a session in its own right. For instance:

1 *Progressive breathing* Awareness is taken to different parts of the body. The person breathes in relaxation and breathes out tension from that part.

2 *Counting* The person counts 'one' and breathes in and 'two' and breathes out, and so on, relaxing with every breath and every number.

3 *Wave imagery* The person is floating in a lake. As they breathe in and out they feel ripples of water against their body and relax more and more.

9 Visualization

Introduction

As anyone who has undertaken relaxation will know, relaxing the body is one thing; being able to control the perpetual stream of chatter that is our mental background is another. The mind likes to be occupied; the more we try to calm it down the more it fights back. It is virtually impossible to calm the mind by the use of the will: "I *will* relax my mind." Few people can manage this for more than a minute or so and, even then, is this forced control really relaxation?

We therefore need techniques which specifically relax the mind; which, moreover, use the mind to relax itself. In Chapter 7 we touched on this with the use of images to enhance physical relaxation. Now we will examine mental relaxation in more depth.

• • • Visualization: Key Points

In visualization we use the faculty of imagination. This is an extremely powerful tool, one which we develop as children and then often fail to use. In terms of relaxation it has three main uses:

1 The imagination is creative, it gives the mind ideas to play with which prevents it from getting bored and sabotaging the session.

2 By focusing on relaxing images we reinforce the fact that we are in a safe environment, which allows us to deepen our physical relaxation.

3 The imagination has a hot line to the unconscious mind, which over time will absorb the relaxing images, enabling the person to become calmer and more relaxed in their everyday lives.

Many of the images used in visualization are based on sensation: that is, sight, touch, taste, smell, hearing and emotional feeling. A scene will be created which suggests what the person will see, the textures they might feel, scents they can smell, sounds they can hear and, more rarely, things they can taste. A relevant mood will be suggested, such as contentment, serenity or perfect peace. The idea is to make the situation as real and absorbing as possible. Most people find visualizing extremely pleasurable; it recaptures some of the openness and wonder of childhood.

The common theme to these sensations is that they are relaxing and uplifting. They focus on such qualities as peace, calm, stillness, beauty, safety, happiness, contentment and tranquillity. The imagination is used to create an alternative, peaceful, reality to our daily lives. Nor is this 'just imagination'. Ideas start in our imaginations, but are actually the blueprints for all that we do and accomplish. If we can change our ideas, we change our lives.

Relaxing images tend to focus on the natural world and idealized scenes. Some trainers suggest using images from the person's everyday lives, for instance a particularly happy holiday, but there are risks in this, since it is a small way from imagining that perfect walk on the beach to remembering how your partner got drunk on sangria and threw up in the swimming pool. Imagined events, by contrast, have a purity which is not contaminated by reality.

• • • Cautions

With the body relaxed and the mind relaxing, the individual is in an extremely receptive state. When people are new to visualization it may be wise to find out if anyone has any deep fears. For instance, someone who is afraid of heights might not appreciate being sent across a blue sky on a pink, fluffy cloud. Rather than lying back relaxing, they may be clinging to the sides with white knuckles! Water and enclosed spaces are other possible problem areas. Generally only strong phobias need to be taken into account. Care should be taken not to *suggest* there may be areas of anxiety when people might not have felt there was a problem. It is useful to get relevant information before the person comes to your class.

Visualization is accessible to everyone. The main group of people who have difficulties with it are those who expect to see perfect images as if on a television screen and are then disappointed. The trainer needs to explain that people's imaginations operate in different ways. Some people are in fact 'visual' and see imagined things as if they were real. Many more get vague impressions and snatches of images. Other people have tactile or auditory imaginations. Alternatively those who operate predominantly on an intellectual level may relate to words better than to images.

These people may be better mentally repeating what is said, rather than trying to imagine anything.

At the end of any visualization it is important to 'return' the person to where they started. If they have gone on a journey, it is customary to return them to the starting-place. If they have been counted down, the trainer can count them back up in the following way:

Three … preparing to become fully alert and awake … two, becoming more and more conscious, feel the life and energy flowing through your body … one … fully alert.

• • • Deepeners

As the name implies, these are techniques which help people to go into a deeper state of relaxation. We have already come across some deepening methods in images used to enhance physical relaxation. Here the techniques are more elaborate and are used to take the person from physical to mental relaxation. They are simple visualizations, which usually focus on the whole body rather than parts, and have a repetitive quality which is used to calm the mind. They encapsulate a feeling which represents deepening relaxation: floating, lightness, colour, going down. Often they involve a short journey.

Deepeners can be used between PR and guided visualization, lasting up to five minutes. However they can

Examples of deepeners

Colour	A colour travels like a mist, flowing down the body, relaxing it. As it touches every part they relax more and more, deeper and deeper…
Counting down	Count the client down slowly from 10 to 1. With every number they are relaxing more and more. At number 1 they achieve complete relaxation.
Descending	They are standing in a garden at the top of a flight of steps. They walk down the steps, relaxing more and more. Count them down. The bottom step is complete relaxation.
Words on a screen	They imagine a screen in their mind's eye. In big letters they write the word 'Peace' and absorb the feeling. They replace 'Peace' with 'Calm', 'Serene' and so on.
Vase of flowers	They fill a vase with a variety of beautiful flowers. With every new flower they relax more deeply. When the vase is full they achieve complete relaxation.
Flying	Lying back, they relax into a soft, pink, fluffy cloud which floats across the sky.
Floating	Lying back ,they relax into a boat, slowly crossing a lake. Their hand trails in the water. They let go completely.
Affirmation	They repeat silently and mentally, "I am relaxing more and more", "I am in perfect harmony."

also stand alone as techniques in their own right. For instance, after PR a deepener could be followed by 10 minutes of listening to music, or in a short session could be the main form of mental relaxation.

• • • Guided Visualizations

Guided visualizations follow the same principles as the deepeners. They are, however, more complicated, involving more of the senses and a detailed journey or experience. At intervals in the visualization it is useful to repeat suggestions which link it with relaxation: for instance, reminders that the body is still letting go, that the breathing is still slowing down.

Other suggestions for visualizations include meadows, mountains, sunsets, rainbows—the list is endless. It is important to be able to generate your own visualizations and use your imagination. Most experienced relaxation trainers can produce images with no reference to any previously prepared script.

Examples of guided visualizations

Woodland walk	You are walking through a wood ... old trees ... sunlight on the leaves ... colours of summer ... smell of earth ... bird song ... ferns swaying in the breeze ... a hot day, but cool in the shade of the trees ... you come to a clearing ... soft lush grass ... you sit down in the shade ... watch the trees ... the sky is blue above you ... rabbits play in the grass, unconcerned by your presence ... you see a fawn; it too is unafraid ... the fawn comes over to you ... you look into its brown, trusting eyes ... it allows you to stroke it, then lies down by your side ... you relax completely ...
Tropical beach	It is a beautiful sunny day. You are on a beach in a tropical paradise ... blue sea, gentle waves sweeping the shore ... golden sand ... you are barefoot, it is soft between your toes ... flowing clothes ... freedom ... shells of luminescent colours ... flying fishes sparkle in the sunlight ... palm trees sway ... you sit down and feel your body sinking back in warm sand ... feel it run through your fingers ... you relax completely ...
Crystal cave	You are on a sunny beach ... you feel hot and enter a cave ... to your surprise it is not dark inside: the walls are made of beautiful sparkling crystal ... the first chamber is made of red crystal which flashes like rubies ... you stay and absorb the colour ... the second is orange ... the third yellow ... the fourth green ... the fifth blue ... the sixth violet, the seventh pearlized white with flashes of other colours ...
Perfect garden	You go down the steps and enter your perfect garden... favourite flowers in beds... smell the scents... see the colours... the grass is green and lush... walk barefoot... a waterfall: hear the sound of the water bubbling and cascading over the rocks... you sit by the pool and listen to the sound of the water...

• • • Pathworking

As people become more experienced in visualizing, more can be left to their imagination. For instance, in the garden relaxation above, rather than the trainer filling the beds with chrysanthemums and lupins, people can be left to imagine their own flowers. Some visualizations rely heavily on the client and are little more than a series of questions: 'You enter a castle ... what does it look like? ... you go into a room ... what do you see?'

If the guided visualization is a holiday for the mind, pathworkings are action holidays. These usually involve a journey of some kind in which people have to make choices. Rather than passively listening they have to participate actively in their fantasy. Pathworkings are often used as a therapeutic tool to explore the unconscious. For instance, a person might dive down into the ocean to bring back an object from a treasure chest. The object would then be discussed with the therapist. In relaxation sessions, however, the focus is on deepening the relaxation session, or finding a method to take it into everyday life. The item from the treasure chest, for example, could be something which represents relaxation to them.

Examples of pathworking

The safe place	A relaxing scene is described, then it is suggested to the person that they find a place where they really feel safe. For an inexperienced group, further suggestions can be made: a bank next to a stream, a country cottage and so on. Alternatively they are left to imagine their own place: the trainer just reinforces the mood by asking open questions and suggesting that they feel perfectly safe, at peace and so on.
Peace in the world	The world is imagined as a globe in the centre of the room. Coloured rays are directed at the globe, sending positive qualities such as peace, love and healing. Participants choose where to send the rays.
Going with the flow	Walking along a river bank, you feel tired and heavy as if your negative emotions are weighing you down. You decide to leave your anger beside the river, or throw it in and let it dissolve away. You walk on feeling lighter and energized. The process is repeated with fear, worry, guilt, envy and so on until you feel so light you could float. You step into the water; it is warm and supportive. For a moment you cling to the bank, then you let go and float downstream in the beautiful, blue, healing waters of the river.
Your guide	This is similar to 'The safe place', except that you are invited to meet your personal guide (or guardian angel) — someone who loves you unconditionally and has your best interests at heart.

••• Affirmations

The relaxed state makes people extremely receptive to suggestions to improve their ability to relax. Affirmations are simple statements which the individual repeats, silently and mentally. The most famous example of an affirmation was developed by Coué, a French pharmacist, early this century: "Every day, in every way, I am getting better and better." Examples include:

I am at perfect peace

Any time I want to relax I can return to this place

I radiate with love

I can relax at will

I am relaxing more and more

Affirmations are made in the present tense. They are positive — "I am relaxing perfectly" — rather than "I am no longer tense." The phrasing should be appropriate to the individual. It is helpful to tell clients they need not go with your suggestion, but can make their own. The person should accompany the phrase with a strong feeling of positive energy to reinforce its power.

Affirmations are often used in the closing stages of a relaxation session, with the purpose of taking the sense of these affirmations into the person's everyday life.

10 Meditation

Introduction

We know that most people's minds are messy jumbles of thoughts, ideas and feelings. Negative self-talk runs riot. Fears, worries, hopes and dreams contend with each other for our mental space. For some people things have got out of control, and seriously affect their personal well-being and ability to cope with life. Meditation is a method of stilling the mind which, once mastered, gives the individual the ability to control thoughts and emotions.

••• Concentration, Meditation and Relaxation

The term 'meditation' tends to be used in a loose way. The aim of people starting out with meditation is really to be able to concentrate. Through focusing on an object, a particular state of mind is developed so that any thoughts, feelings or sensations which are experienced are not given any interest, and therefore die away. Once the mind is able to concentrate for longer periods of time the individual starts to meditate. This involves a feeling of inner peace and calm. In advanced states of meditation the experience deepens so that there is an altered state of consciousness, usually associated with feelings of love and connectedness with the universe.

The state of mind in meditation is similar to, but not identical with, that in deep relaxation. With meditation there is more alertness and awareness, exemplified by the fact that it is done sitting up, so energy can flow through the spine. The focus is very much on the use of the mind, while the body does not relax as deeply as, for example, in progressive relaxation (PR). Research indicates that the health benefits of meditation are similar to those of other relaxation methods. Mental benefits are more far-reaching. Concentration is very empowering; it enables people to have control over their minds, perhaps for the first time. True meditation involves living in the present moment and thus freeing oneself from worries of past and future. There is a sense of space, quite unusual in our frenetic life style.

Prejudice against Meditation

Anyone teaching meditation to the general public will find that a few people are dubious about, even fearful of meditation. If they have no previous knowledge of the subject they may have picked up that it is a strange eastern religion, or associated with hippies and drug users. These people can be reassured that meditation is a technique of mind control which can be practised separate from any religious connections. It can also fit in perfectly well with any religious beliefs that an individual may have. For instance prayer can be seen as a form of meditation. You will find, however, that many evangelical Christians will be unwilling to undertake meditation.

Safe Practice

The information in this book will equip you to undertake an 'Introduction to Meditation' session which involves brief, 'taster' exercises. If you wish to pursue teaching meditation in more depth, you are strongly advised to study with one of the many reputable organizations which now offer training courses.

Occasionally, even with only five minutes' concentration, an individual experiences discomfort and anxiety, usually to do with thoughts that they cannot control rushing into their minds. It is then up to both of you to decide whether it is worth pursuing the technique, or whether the time is not right. Meditation can bring to the surface suppressed emotions, much in the same way as relaxation techniques, and you need to be able to deal with these. However, in contrast, I have found that some people are more comfortable with meditation than with relaxation. They say that the meditation exercises give their minds something to do, and that they prefer them to lying passive. One man, for instance, got no benefit from any other relaxation technique, but found that staring at a candle was extremely calming for him.

It is also worth noting that meditation can have a very powerful effect on a few people. A minority, for instance, have strong experiences or sensations such as colours, scenes and even the presence of other beings. This is extremely unlikely to happen in a five-minute meditation in a class setting. However some people may do longer sessions on their own and find themselves facing these experiences. If they are disturbed rather than intrigued by this, they will need help. Advice can be sought from experienced meditation teachers. At this stage it probably needs to be pointed out that the most worrying thing most budding meditators experience is an overwhelming desire to nod off!

Physical Posture

This is as outlined in Section six (page 29). It must be emphasized that the spine should be kept upright. Just as in relaxation, the eyes are usually closed. However some schools advocate that the eyes be kept half open and cast down to the floor. This can be quite a useful adaptation, particularly for people inclined to doze.

An Object on which to Concentrate

This can be material — a physical object, such as a flower — or abstract — a concept or idea, such as peace.

Attitude of Mind

This is at the basis of successful meditation. The aim is to concentrate, but any idea of force or will power is the opposite of what we are trying to achieve. Inevitably, after a short period of time, our minds will wander from our object of concentration. If this happens we remain passive observers. We observe what is happening in our minds and do not get hooked into it. We watch it die away through lack of interest, then we are able to return to our object. Attention is given, without any analysis, judgement, comparison or criticism: in short, *pure awareness*. A particularly important point is not to get irritated with oneself when the mind strays. Irritation simply compounds the problem. If we feel this stirring, we need to let it go and return to the object of concentration.

Helpful Images

The following suggestions may be given to people to give them a 'feel' for what they are trying to achieve:

Clear a space in the mind as wide as the sky.

The mind is like an ocean with the thoughts like waves; feel the waves calming down until the ocean is still. Thoughts in the mind are like ripples which gently die away.

Relax the mind. Let thoughts come and go; you are not interested in them.

Release tension. Your mind is like an animal wandering and lost. Gently bring your mind home.

Preparation

Preparation greatly aids meditation. It provides a transition between the outside world and the inner world the person is about to enter. A useful preparation is to do a quick mental PR or a breathing exercise at the start of the session.

Just as people find certain forms of relaxation more appropriate for them, so it may be useful to choose a meditation technique which feels right for the individual.

Visual Meditations

In visual meditations the eyes are kept soft and relaxed. They should not be over-focused.

1 The candle flame A lighted candle is placed in front of the individual, who is encouraged to watch the flame and become absorbed in it.

2 A flower The person observes the flower, taking in its shape and colour, texture and size.

Any uplifting object can be used as an object for meditation. Other examples include crystals, plants, paintings, ornaments and abstract designs. If the person wishes to shut their eyes they can visualize the object mentally.

Mantra Meditations

A mantra is a word or phrase which is repeated over and over, either in the mind or, less commonly, out loud. The most famous mantra is the hindu 'Om', pronounced 'aum', which is said to be the original sound of the universe. However any positive word or phrase can be a mantra. Suggestions include 'Peace', 'Love', 'Light' and 'Be here now'.

Breath Meditations

The individual takes their attention to their breath. They watch the breath going in and the breath going out. They simply observe. At the same time the mind might be focused on the tip of the nose where the air enters and leaves, or on the 'hara' centre, approximately two inches below the navel. (The hara is the centre of gravity used in martial arts and gives a powerful focus for the breath. Care should be taken not to expand the stomach on the in breath if focusing on this point.)

Alternatively the breath is counted as it is observed. For instance, in breaths could be 'one' and out breaths 'two'. Another method is to count up to a set number, say 50 or 100.

Music Meditations

Classical, ethnic or new age music is best for this. The person allows their minds to follow the flow of the music.

Visualizations for Meditation

Many of the images in Section 9, if simplified, are suitable for meditation. Also useful are the following:

1 *Sun, moon and stars* The individual visualizes the sun casting light in a blue sky; the moon, pale and serene in the night sky; the stars bright and sparkling in the darkness.

2 *The river* A river is visualized, a constant flow of water across the countryside.

3 *Colours* The mind is filled with a colour which dissipates to be replaced by another.

4 *Inner smile* A beautiful smile is imagined and felt. The smile is placed in the mind and focused on. It can also be moved around to parts of the body.

The
Application
of Relaxation

3

11 Common Problems Encountered in Relaxation Training

Introduction

In this chapter we look at some of the common problems you may encounter when running relaxation sessions and give a range of solutions that can be used. A useful guide to the scenarios listed below are that, the more serious the problem, the less likely you are to experience it. For instance, in 15 years of teaching relaxation, I have never experienced anyone becoming ill during a relaxation session. On the other hand, the more minor, disruptive problems are quite likely to happen.

• • • Disruptions Outside the Session

A Disturbing Level of Noise Outside Your Room

Your setting will obviously govern how much control you have over this. Noises I have experienced include the following: building work being done (workers seem to be able to time their drilling to coincide with the exact half-hour you want for relaxation); people talking, screaming, shouting or partying outside the room; noise from other groups, as when a class next door is using the video; fire drills; people popping their heads round the door, saying, "Oh, sorry" and closing the door with a slam or, worse, trying to start a conversation oblivious to the drawn curtains and prone bodies surrounding you!

At the same time disruptions may be subjective in nature. For instance, the trainer, who wants things to go right, may be hypersensitive to any sound outside the room, while the participants themselves may not notice anything. Alternatively you may find that people are driven mad by the buzz of the central heating system, which you have not even heard. Music can often be used to drown out slight background noise.

The important thing to realize is that people cannot relax in the middle of disruption. If things become too bad it will be necessary to find another venue.

Planning and Negotiation

While some situations will be unavoidable crises, many of the above problems can be avoided by planning. This involves reminding everyone around that your session is about to happen and you need quiet for the next half-hour. If you are likely to be disturbed, a prominent sign on the door is a good idea. If this is too subtle, a free-standing sign that people have to walk around may work. Even if your session happens at the same time every week, other people may forget it and think it is a good idea to test the fire alarms, so make your presence felt.

Negotiation should be used with colleagues — you are very much dependent on the good will of the teacher next door as to whether they are willing to put their video on at another time. Again, if this is the sort of situation which often arises, it is best to address it before the session starts.

• • • Disruptions Within the Session

Giggling and Laughing

It is not uncommon for someone to giggle, then perhaps for the whole group to dissolve into hysterics. My personal opinion is that laughter is a great discharger of stress and that the whole group will feel much better for it. Indeed laughter even massages the internal organs. In this situation I would let the laughter take its course and die down naturally, then I would carry on with the relaxation.

Habitual gigglers will be a problem. You will need to discuss with them what is going on. Perhaps they do not wish to be involved in relaxation and are using this as passive resistance; or it may be caused by anxiety, in which case individual relaxation may be helpful until they feel more at ease.

Snorers and Coughers

Snorers come in all shapes and sizes, and both sexes, and are generally very disruptive. It is impossible to relax when waiting to see whether their next breath will be an eardrum blaster or a cosy little snuffle. Snorers cause giggling and eventually exasperation. They themselves may be embarrassed; sometimes people will not take part in relaxation because they know they have this problem. The solution is to prevent the snorer from falling asleep, which after all is not the aim of relaxation. Posture goes a long way towards this. A block under the head may help; sitting in a chair nearly always works. Alternatively the person could keep their eyes open. The same positions could be adopted for people who are coughing. A glass of water could also be put close to hand. *It would be extremely dangerous to suck cough sweets when relaxing.*

Leaving the Room

Sometimes people have had enough and wish to leave the session. It is far better to let this happen than to have a restless, anxious person disturb the rest of the group. However it is useful to have as a ground rule of the group that people who need to leave do so quietly, and that they do not come back into the room.

• • • Clients Experiencing Problems

Crying

Relaxation can be a very powerful experience for some people. Sometimes when they switch off their minds, they may get in touch with deep emotions, so that crying is not uncommon. If someone is crying you may feel it is sufficient to ask them quietly whether they want to leave the room and have some time to themselves. However, if the person is very distressed, you will need to interrupt the session. This can be done with minimal disruption by telling the group, "For the next few minutes you can continue to relax in silence. Any noise that you hear will not disturb you. You are completely at peace with yourself."

You can then accompany the person from the room, and assess whether they need to be on their own or to talk to someone. Ideally another staff member can be used for this. If no one is available you will have to balance this person's needs with those of the group. Your alternatives are to finish the group quickly, or, if they are experienced, to tell them they can relax for a set length of time and to ask someone in the group to act as timekeeper.

Remember that some emotional crises can in fact be breakthroughs for the person and that they need to be supported effectively. However, if someone habitually cries in a group, it will be necessary to address why this is happening and possibly to arrange individual sessions.

Panic Attacks/Hyperventilation/Feeling of Choking/Claustrophobia

My most horrible experience when taking a relaxation session was when a woman began to hyperventilate and go into a panic attack. Through her gasps she could only manage to tell me that she had started to go down a deep black hole. Luckily it was in an individual session and, sounding rather than feeling calm, I encouraged her to take deep breaths and talked her back into reality. In retrospect I often wonder what could have been achieved if I had had the confidence to help her to explore that black hole.

If people suffer from any of the above conditions your actions could be similar to those used for people who cry in the session. Someone claustrophobic, for example, may feel better just by being able to move and leave the room. It can also be helpful to position them by the door. However some people may need to be taken from the group and, in extreme circumstances, it may be better to move the group from round them. Either yourself or another staff member needs to sit with them. Reassure them, encourage them to breathe normally and allow them to talk about what is happening for them. If this should be a recurrent problem then, again, the alternative of individual sessions would need to be looked at.

A first aid cure for hyperventilation is to get the person to breathe four or five times into a paper bag. This cuts down on the over-absorption of oxygen caused by over-breathing. All the above conditions are likely to be distressing, but not serious. However, from the first aid point of view, it is necessary to assess whether there is a medical problem involved. If in doubt ask the person to consult their doctor.

It is extremely useful for anyone delivering relaxation training to take a First Aid Certificate.

Slowness in Waking Up

My second most horrible experience was the first time a solidly unmoving figure lay silent on the floor, resisting all my encouragements of "You are now waking up and opening your eyes." I felt slightly better when I saw that the individual was still breathing, but this was replaced by the worry that they were never going to wake up.

It is not in fact unusual for people to go into a deep sleep in relaxation, particularly if they have problems sleeping at other times, and if they are on medication. Repeat the instructions to wake up several times, firmly. If this does not work you will now need to assess the person in the light of your knowledge of them. My personal preference is to leave them to sleep it off and wake up naturally, perhaps leaving a light on in the room so they do not wake up and panic, wondering where they are. If there are concerns about the individual, someone could stay with them. If it is essential, then the person can be touched gently, on shoulder or arm. Don't worry, they will wake up eventually!

Cramp

Occasionally someone may experience cramp through lying awkwardly in one position for a long time. Cramps are helped by stretching strongly and/or massaging the affected area.

Epilepsy

I have never come across anyone experiencing an epileptic fit while in relaxation. On the contrary the darkened, quiet room will have a beneficial effect. I did, however, know one person who rejoined a noisy, brightly lit room too quickly after relaxation and had a fit.

The procedure for epileptic fits is to clear away any obstacles that might do the person some harm. When the fit is over, lay the person on their side in the recovery position, as described in first aid handbooks, check the air passages for blockages and remove false teeth. When they are awake check to see they have not injured themselves by their fall, and whether they need help cleaning up if they have evacuated bladder or bowel.

Breathing Problems

People who have breathing problems such as asthma may find breathing exercises in relaxation uncomfortable. This is often because they associate breathing with feelings of panic and discomfort. It is better to avoid reference to breathing with such people. However they can certainly benefit from learning correct respiration methods, possibly through yoga, which is the main discipline which teaches about breathing. Once they feel more easy with their breathing, they may be happy to use it to relax.

If you have any concerns about a group member's medical condition advise this person to consult a general practitioner. In an emergency, call an ambulance.

12 Relaxation with Different Client Groups

Introduction

While the relaxation techniques outlined in Part 2 are suitable for most client groups, different sets of people will have particular relaxation needs. This chapter indicates some approaches to relaxation which can be of use with different client groups.

• • • People with Mental Health Problems

Relaxation is most commonly used for people with mental health problems. It can be suitable for the entire range of problems, from people who are experiencing life stress to those who are diagnosed as having long-term problems such as schizophrenia, provided the individual is sufficiently stable emotionally. Physical relaxation such as PR can be more appropriate than visualization for people who experience distortions of reality.

With people with mental health problems you are likely to come across some of the issues discussed in the previous section, such as panic in the session, agitation and emotional issues coming to the surface. The following problems are also commonly experienced.

Participants Who Will not Stay in the Session

It is quite usual to come across a number of people who cannot stay in relaxation sessions. They say that they find relaxation uncomfortable, they cannot stay still for this length of time, their minds are full of disturbing thoughts, they cannot let go. Such people often benefit more from relaxation techniques which are active in nature, such as yoga, tai chi and massage. This is also a clear indication that they have issues which need to be addressed.

Problems Associated with Medication

While the main problem for people on medication is that they are likely to be sleepy during relaxation, a small number complain that their medication is making them agitated so they cannot relax. There are in fact a number of conditions in which medication causes people to be agitated.

The antipsychotic drugs can induce a condition known as 'Paradoxical Excitement' in which the person experiences the opposite effect to what the drug intended. This happens in less than 10 per cent of people. A similar number can be effected by tricyclic antidepressants, with an effect similar to taking in too much caffeine. In early stages of treatment a similar effect may be experienced by people on the SSRI antidepressants.

Finally a condition known as akathisia can be an effect of some antipsychotic drugs. This produces a feeling of intense internal discomfort, which means the person has to be continually on the move to try and stop this feeling.

If any of the above are suspected the individual should be referred back to the family doctor or psychiatrist.

••• Disabled People

It is necessary to spend some time with disabled people prior to their first session to find out their particular needs and how you can help with these. The following are some typical situations.

Mobility Problems

Wheelchairs are rarely suitable for relaxation. If possible, help the person transfer to another chair. Many people in wheelchairs can get down to the floor with some support. This can be a real achievement and can promote confidence. The individual should stand and lean their hands on a stout chair in front of them. They kneel down with one leg, then the other, then guide their weight down to the ground. To get up they reverse the procedure.

People with Hearing Disabilities

People who have partial hearing should be positioned close to you. Personal stereos with music or your recorded scripts may be helpful for some. For those with profound hearing disability, time needs to be allowed for them to go over and memorize their own, written relaxation script. Individual time will be needed to undertake demonstration of the principles of techniques such as PR. Some people are sensitive to percussion noises, such as drums, which with some creativity could be used to create a relaxing rhythm. Coloured lights and crystals could be used as visual means of promoting relaxation. Alternatively the less verbal forms of relaxation, meditation, yoga and massage will be useful.

People with Visual Disabilities

People with visual disabilities do not normally have special needs in relaxation, most of which, after all, is done with the eyes closed. For people who have been unable to see from birth it may be useful to check their understanding of such things as colour, and whether you should change your imagery to something more appropriate to them. You will of course need to be alert to the needs of individuals when movement is required at the start and end of the session. If any posture work is done, the trainer will need to explain this in great detail, and possibly to use their hands to adjust positions.

• • • Children

In general children are very open to relaxation. Their flexible minds and access to imagination make them very effective subjects. If the session is seen as enjoyable they will be keen to continue.

Toddlers and Young Children

Rooms such as the Snoezelen can be useful for preschool children who will be stimulated by the simple sensory effects. Twinkling lights, bubbles, music and fragrances, can all produce a relaxing effect if introduced calmly. Relaxation can follow gentle exercise, to damp down too high spirits. Particularly effective are gentle massage and soothing physical contact, such as holding or cuddling.
NB Please refer to the rules of your organization about physical contact with clients.

Older Children

Older children are able to respond to the more creative forms of relaxation. They are easily bored, so the session should contain a lot of variety. Particularly effective are creative visualizations which will come across to children like a story. This is a good chance for the trainer to really let go and use their imagination. Care must be taken with the presentation of these or else, instead of relaxing in a castle on a distant planet, the children will be fighting Klingons. Particularly useful for children are topics which always interest them, such as animals, exploring, space, the sea, special powers and secret places.

Children in a group can be disruptive. It is important to set a routine whereby, the minute they enter the room, relaxation is expected. Have the room ready prepared, and lead them to expect that this is no occasion to mess around.

With some children individual relaxation may be more appropriate.

Hyperactive Children

Individual relaxation may be attempted. However the more physical forms of relaxation, particularly massage, may be more effective.

Adolescents

Adolescents can use all the relaxation techniques suitable for adults. The main problems likely to be faced are that they do not appreciate the need for relaxation, lack motivation and a feeling of embarrassment in doing anything out of the ordinary.

Mixed-sex relaxation groups are not particularly successful because of feelings of unease and embarrassment. Even single-sex groups may have problems if not all the participants are well motivated. Individual sessions may then be the best option.

• • • People with Learning Disabilities and People with Dementia

Suitable relaxation techniques for these people depend upon their level of understanding. People with severe disabilities will benefit most from simple stimulation, such as from Snoezelen equipment and massage, as for young children.

The more able will be able to undertake PR and creative visualization. The trainer must be careful to match the session to the level of ability. It may take longer to explain the principles of relaxation and the trainer should be prepared to go at the pace of participants and repeat where necessary. It can be helpful to demonstrate relaxation rather than simply giving instructions. Generally small groups or individual work are more appropriate. Topics should be related to interest. Older people, for instance, could be taken to scenes from an earlier age. Many specialist learning disability units now have access to a Snoezelen. Care should be taken that these are used as part of a regular programme of relaxation. If they are used in response to challenging behaviour, it is not unknown for people who enjoy the Snoezelen to play up, in order to get extra time in there! In this case prevention is better than reward.

The Relaxation Course

4

Introduction

1 To present a number of different relaxation methods
from which individual participants can choose the
techniques which work best for them.
2 To enable people to develop skills in relaxation
techniques and become more relaxed in their everyday
lives.

. . . Objectives

By the end of the course people will be able to:

- understand and use relaxation techniques including
progressive relaxation, breathing, differential relaxation,
visualization and meditation;
- be aware of the difference between tension and
relaxation in their bodies;
- understand the benefits of relaxation;
- establish a suitable environment and routine for
relaxation;
- select relaxation techniques which are most beneficial
for them.

. . . Format

Number of sessions Eight
Size of group Six to twelve people
Duration Two hours a week for eight weeks
Content A mixture of discussion, exercises and handouts.
Home exercises are suggested for each week so people can
practise their skills. Session plans are a *guide* for facilitators
and should be adapted to suit the needs of the group.
Opening and closing the circle Each session starts with an
exercise which is suitable to relax people and encourage
them to talk. Sessions end with an exercise which is positive
and fun. In these exercises the facilitator goes round the
circle giving each person a turn.
Equal time Pair exercises are based on the principle of equal
time. They are not conversations, rather each person has
half the time allotted in which to talk, while the other
person encourages them, without talking about themselves.
The facilitator keeps time.

Writing Any exercises involving writing are entirely voluntary. The facilitator should discreetly check whether people have problems with reading or writing.

Role of the facilitator The facilitator's role is to encourage communication, impart information and keep the group on target. The facilitator may join in exercises, especially the opening and closing circle, and share information about themselves, where relevant.

Confidentiality This is a rule which is binding on all participants. No one, including the facilitator, should refer to *anything* a group member has said in the group, outside the session, unless that person brings the issue up themselves. People should only share what they feel comfortable with. If your organization has its own rules with regard to confidentiality these should be shared at the beginning of the group.

1 Body Awareness

• • • Objectives

By the end of the session participants will:

- understand and practise the difference between tension and relaxation;
- understand the reasons why we experience physical tension;
- get to know the other participants and the facilitator.

Plan

Welcome	Facilitator introduces self. Practical information about toilets, fire exits, breaks, smoking arrangements and so on. Outline of what people can expect from the course: aims, objectives, sessions, format.	***(10 minutes)***
Names and introductory exercise	People go round circle saying their names. In pairs they discuss why they wanted to do this course and what they want to achieve from it. Pairs share this information with the group, once again saying their names.	***(20 minutes)*** *(10 minutes)* *(10 minutes)*
Handout	**Physical Tension Checklist** This is given to each participant to fill in individually. Facilitator encourages group discussion.	***(15 minutes)*** *(5 minutes)* *(10 minutes)*
Exercise	**Postures** Facilitator demonstrates suitable postures for relaxation, gets people to try these and checks for special needs.	***(15 minutes)***
Break	....	***(10 minutes)***
Handout	**Tension and Relaxation** Facilitator distributes handout and goes through it, encouraging discussion.	***(10 minutes)***

Awareness of physical tension *(25 minutes)*

Participants lie on the floor or sit in a chair. Facilitator goes through the parts of the body, as in PR, asking people what tension they can feel there.

Feedback

The exercise is repeated, this time stretching and relaxing some body parts.

Feedback

Awareness of physical tension *(5 minutes)*

Participants are asked to spend time over the next week being aware of any particular areas of their body which are prone to tension, and of any situations which make them particularly tense.

Your most relaxing holiday. *(10 minutes)*

Physical Tension Checklist

Physical tension can show itself in a number of ways.
See how many of the following signs of physical tension
you feel apply to you.

1

HANDOUT

	Never	Occasionally	Often

Muscle Tension

	Never	Occasionally	Often
Face	☐	☐	☐
Jaw	☐	☐	☐
Neck	☐	☐	☐
Shoulders	☐	☐	☐
Stomach	☐	☐	☐
Hands/fingers	☐	☐	☐
Back	☐	☐	☐
Buttocks	☐	☐	☐
Feet	☐	☐	☐

Other _____

Breathing Problems

	Never	Occasionally	Often
Shallow breathing	☐	☐	☐
Panting/gasping breath	☐	☐	☐
Forgetting to breathe	☐	☐	☐
Hyper-ventilation	☐	☐	☐
Panicky breathing	☐	☐	☐
Out of breath	☐	☐	☐

General Signs

	Never	Occasionally	Often
Headaches	☐	☐	☐
Dizziness	☐	☐	☐
Skin conditions	☐	☐	☐
Watery eyes	☐	☐	☐
High blood pressure	☐	☐	☐
Feel of irregular heartbeat	☐	☐	☐
Needing the lavatory	☐	☐	☐
Feeling hot and sweaty	☐	☐	☐

General Conditions

	Never	Occasionally	Often
Disturbed appetite	☐	☐	☐
Sleep patterns disturbed	☐	☐	☐
Feeling tired and without energy	☐	☐	☐
Feeling uncoordinated	☐	☐	☐
Feeling restless and agitated	☐	☐	☐

Stress-related illness _____

Other signs _____

HANDOUT 1

Tension and Relaxation

••• Physical Tension

Simple observation of other people shows how many of us carry round large amounts of physical tension. The posture in which we sit is likely to be slumped, putting strain on the spine and internal organs. The way in which we walk may be lopsided or stiff.

As we grow older most of us become so accustomed to this tension that we are unaware that it is there. Common areas in which we hold tension are the shoulders (hunched and raised), the stomach (knotted) and the face (frowning, clenching the jaw, chewing the mouth). However tension can be lurking in practically every area of the body.

••• Causes of Tension

It is generally agreed that unwanted tension comes from the misuse of the 'fight or flight' mechanism. This is the name for the physiological changes which occur when we experience a threatening situation. For instance, if we are facing danger our breathing becomes faster and shallower to enable quicker absorption of oxygen, our heart rate increases and our blood pressure rises so that the lungs and muscles are primed for action, our muscles tense, ready to move. All these changes are autonomic — beyond our conscious control. It has been found that the stresses of modern life can put people into 'fight or flight' mode inappropriately. Queue jumpers, arguments with the family or disputes at work can all activate our bodies for physical action which will be inappropriate in these situations. Some people who face a lot of stress may unknowingly be in 'fight or flight' mode most of the time!

••• Effects of Tension

These unwanted physical changes will have a negative effect on our bodies, causing many of the signs of physical tension, and in some cases leading to stress-related illness, such as high blood pressure, stomach disorders and arguably, cancer.

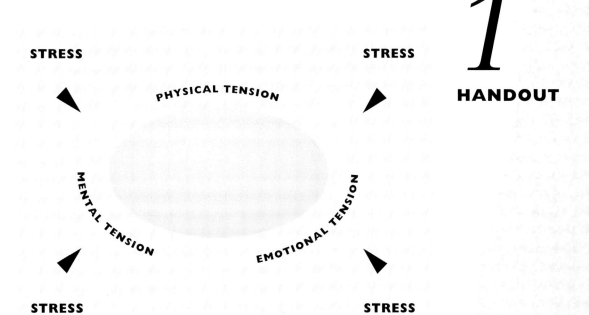

STRESS   STRESS

PHYSICAL TENSION

MENTAL TENSION   EMOTIONAL TENSION

STRESS   STRESS

• • • Three Types of Tension

As well as physical tension we often suffer from mental and emotional tension, such as mood swings, worry, forgetfulness and getting things out of proportion. When we are faced by outside stress, such as pressure at work or relationship problems, these three types can interact and reinforce each other, leading to severe stress problems.

• • • The Role of Relaxation

Relaxation techniques are a way of releasing unwanted tension by gaining control over the autonomic nervous system. By consciously letting go of tension from the muscles, and creating an environment which is safe and quiet, our bodies naturally go from activated into de-activated mode. Similarly, mental relaxation techniques work directly on releasing mental tension and, because the mental, physical and emotional are all connected, also enhance physical relaxation.

    Relaxation has a number of benefits. Physically we will become relaxed and easy, so that many of the physical signs of tension will disappear. Our health is likely to improve. Overall we will be happier, more fulfilled and able to cope with life with ease, rather than struggling with it. Of course we will still face crises and life traumas, but with relaxation our ability to cope with these and move on will be greatly increased.

1

HANDOUT

A particular feature of relaxation techniques, especially those which concentrate on mental relaxation, is that they induce a form of brain wave pattern, known as alpha waves, which are associated with feelings of peace and calm.

Relaxation techniques are extremely effective, proven over many years. There is nothing mysterious or clever about relaxation. It is a skill which practically everyone can learn. Once learnt it needs to be practised consistently until it becomes a way of life, just as we practiced tension so that it became our way of life! It is your choice. Do you choose relaxation or tension?

2 Progressive Relaxation

• • • Objectives

By the end of the session participants will be able to:

- understand and practice PR;
- plan a suitable place and time for their relaxation session.

Equipment: if possible, a progressive relaxation tape should be provided for each person.

Plan

Opening circle	Participants say briefly how they are feeling now.	*(10 minutes)*
Feedback on home exercise	If the group is relaxed, this exercise can be done with the whole group. If not, they can work in pairs, then feed back to the group.	*(10 minutes)*
Handout	**Progressive Relaxation** Facilitator distributes handout, then goes through it, encouraging discussion.	*(15 minutes)*
Exercise	**PR** Facilitator leads a session of PR.	*(20 minutes)*
Break	....	*(10 minutes)*
Feedback on PR exercise	....	*(10 minutes)*
Discussion	**Relaxing at home** Facilitator encourages discussion on the practical issues of relaxing at home, such as how to get peace and quiet, and puts the suggestions on a flip chart.	*(15 minutes)*
Exercise	**Personal PR script** Facilitator reads through personal PR script to participants in relaxation position. Facilitator gives suggestions on how	*(20 minutes)*

people can use their script: memorize the principles, don't worry about details. Facilitator distributes Personal Progressive Relaxation Script handout.

<table>
<tr><td>**Home exercise**</td><td>Participants are to undertake PR, ideally once a day for a week in a relaxing environment, using tape or script.</td><td>*(5 minutes)*</td></tr>
<tr><td>**Closing circle**</td><td>Your most relaxing colour.</td><td>*(5 minutes)*</td></tr>
</table>

Progressive Relaxation

••• Background

Progressive relaxation (PR) was founded in the early years of this century by an American doctor who found that, by the conscious release of tension from the skeletal muscular system, anxiety and stress conditions were greatly improved.

Our muscles are largely under voluntary control. When we relax these, there is a relaxation effect on the rest of the body, including the systems we cannot consciously control, such as the heart and digestion. In short the whole body relaxes.

PR works by first gently stretching and then releasing areas of the body. The action of stretching is inevitably followed by some release, hence relaxation of the part of the body. PR is often used as the basis for other relaxation techniques.

••• Four Stages

There are four stages in PR:

1 *Awareness of tension* We concentrate on a particular area of the body and learn to recognize tension.

2 *Stretching to promote tension* We stretch the area to maximize the tension.

3 *Releasing the stretch* We release the stretch to let go of tension.

4 *Awareness of relaxation* We focus our attention on the particular area of the body and learn to recognize relaxation.

••• Areas of the Body

PR always progresses from feet to head. The order can be: feet, legs, buttocks, pelvis, stomach, back and spine, shoulder blades, chest, hands, arms, shoulders, neck, face (jaw, mouth, cheeks, forehead, eyes, ears, scalp). Options include the internal organs and the skin.

••• The Stretch

This can be firm, but not aggressive, as this would build up more tension. It lasts three to six seconds. Often at the start or end of a session the whole body is stretched and released three times.

HANDOUT

• • • Suggestions

To enhance the relaxation, suggestions are made which encourage release. Words such as 'warmth', 'flowing', 'relaxing', 'releasing', 'letting go', 'lightness', 'heaviness', 'waves', 'softening' or 'floating' can be used.

• • • Methods

PR can be practised at organized classes, by listening to tapes or by personally going through the technique. In the latter, repeating instructions to yourself has a self-hypnotic effect. Alternatively you can record your own tape.

Personal Progressive Relaxation Script

This text gives guidance and suggestions on how to structure and word your relaxation session. It does not have to be memorized or followed word for word. It can be adapted to suit your own needs.

I take my awareness to my left foot. I stretch my left foot by pointing the toes away. I release the stretch and feel relaxation flowing into my left foot. I repeat with the right foot.

My attention is focused on my left leg. I stretch the leg first by raising it six inches from the floor and pointing the toes, then by flexing the foot back. When I release the stretch my left leg is relaxing completely. All the tension is flowing away. I repeat with the right leg.

I take my awareness to my buttocks. I tense these by pressing them close together. I release them and they soften and relax.

I concentrate on my pelvis, stretching it by raising it slightly from the ground and tipping it to the left and right. As I release I feel all the tension flowing from my pelvis.

Now the whole of my body from my feet to my pelvis is starting to release tension and let go. It is starting to relax completely.

My attention flows to my stomach. I tense this by pulling the stomach muscles in tightly and then letting them flop out. I repeat this twice more. My stomach flops, totally letting go of tension. It rises and falls gently with my breathing and relaxes more and more.

I take my attention to the area of my back and spine, and tense it by arching my spine slightly from the ground. I release slowly from the base of my spine, feeling each vertebra being massaged by the floor. My back and spine are relaxing completely. Tension flows away into the floor beneath. The floor is supporting my whole weight as I relax into it.

My awareness moves to my shoulder blades. I stretch these by pushing them gently together, then release so they widen and soften into the floor. My shoulder blades relax completely.

My whole body is relaxing more and more. Tension is flowing away. I feel warm and light and relaxed. Lighter and lighter. More and more relaxed. I am letting go completely.

My mind goes to my chest, which I tense by pushing towards the ceiling and letting go. My chest sinks down but remains open, it relaxes more and more.

I am aware of my arms and my hands, which I tense by raising them a few inches from the ground. As I release and lower them I feel tension flowing down through my arms and out through my fingertips.

I concentrate on my shoulders. I tense these by raising them towards my ears, and let them sink down, feeling the tension flowing away. My shoulders drift down and back towards the floor as they relax more and more.

I relax my neck by raising my head slightly from the floor, chin to chest, and then lowering it gently. All the muscles in my neck are releasing and letting go. If tension remains I move my head gently to left and right and feel it releasing with the movement.

Finally I move my attention to my face and head. I am aware of the tension in my forehead and feel this releasing as if cool fingers were stroking the tension away. The lines on my forehead are being smoothed. This feeling of relaxation flows down over my eyes. Eyelids are gently touching, the tiny muscles are releasing and letting go. My cheeks are softening; inside my closed mouth my lower jaw drops slightly. Relaxation is flowing over the whole of my face; even the tiny muscles around my ears and at the back of my scalp are releasing and letting go.

Now, from the top of my head to the bottom of my feet, my whole body is relaxing and letting go. I feel lighter and lighter, more and more relaxed. All the heaviness gone, I am relaxing completely. All the tension has flowed away, I am softening and relaxing completely...

3 Relaxed Breathing

• • • Objectives

By the end of the session participants will be able to:

- understand the benefits of correct breathing and its relationship with relaxation;
- do the complete breath and variations;
- undertake breathing exercises at home.

Plan

Opening circle — Who is the most tense famous person? *(5 minutes)*

Feedback on home exercise — In pairs, participants discuss how the home exercise went.
In the large group, facilitator leads feedback, concentrating on overcoming difficulties that may have been faced, and what has been gained. *(20 minutes)*

Handout — **Relaxed breathing**
Facilitator distributes and goes through the first part of the handout, including principles of relaxed breathing. Facilitator should enquire whether any people have concerns about breathing exercises. If people are very concerned they can be given the option of observing the exercises. *(15 minutes)*

Exercise — **The complete breath**
Facilitator leads people through this part of the handout, practising the complete breath. *(15 minutes)*

Feedback

Break .... *(10 minutes)*

Breathing in relaxation exercises — Facilitator goes through the last part of the handout. *(10 minutes)*

Mini sessions on breathing exercises	Facilitator leads a couple of exercises based on breathing, such as counting the breath, wave imagery or tension release on exhalation.	*(15 minutes)*
	Feedback	
PR with breathing	Facilitator leads PR exercise with a focus on the breath.	*(20 minutes)*
Home exercise	Participants can replace their daily PR exercise with breathing, or can do a combination, or, if this is preferred, continue with PR alone.	*(5 minutes)*
Closing circle	Who is the most relaxed famous personality?	*(5 minutes)*

The Relaxation Therapy Manual

Relaxed Breathing

Relaxed breathing is a vital part of complete relaxation. Physical tension often shows itself in disturbances in the way we breathe. Common breathing faults include shallow breath, panting, gasping, rigid chest, raising the shoulders, uneven breath and, in some cases, hyperventilation.

Without correct breathing the body is laid open to problems which come from not inhaling sufficient oxygen and not exhaling toxins. These include fatigue, lack of concentration, sleep problems, depression, respiratory problems, digestive disorders, damage to skin, bones, teeth and hair and a general predisposition to illness. However, if we master correct breathing, we will markedly improve our physical health, while the free circulation of energy in the body will bring mental alertness.

In terms of relaxation, the respiratory system is one of the first to be affected by 'fight or flight' activation. However we can consciously relax our breathing, thereby de-activating the whole body.

• • • Principles of Relaxed Breathing

Relaxed breathing is slow, deep, even and easy. It is always done through the nose, rather than the mouth. The breathing apparatus — lungs, diaphragm, ribs and so on — should all be relaxed.

• • • The Complete Breath

The complete breath is a method of breathing that utilizes the whole of the lungs. The breath is taught in three parts: activating the lower lungs by expanding the lower ribs slightly, out and to the side, activating the middle lungs by stretching the mid-rib cage to the side; and activating the upper lungs by raising the breast bone slightly.

Once these stages are mastered, the three are put together into one complete breath. The complete breath is at the same time relaxing and energizing.

• • • Breathing in Relaxation Exercises

Breathing can be used in a number of ways in relaxation:

- it is often used to enhance progressive relaxation. People are encouraged to release tension on the out breath and breathe in relaxation on the inhalation.
- it can also be a relaxation technique in its own right, for instance by using wave imagery to relax more and more with inhalation and exhalation, or by counting the breath.
- it is also a useful relaxation technique in stressful situations, when 'breathing deeply' can prevent activation of 'fight or flight'.

4 Differential Relaxation

••• Objectives

By the end of the session participants will be able to:

- understand the principles of differential relaxation (DR);
- undertake DR in the situations of their choice.

Plan

Opening circle	One nice thing which has happened since last week.	*(5 minutes)*
Feedback on home exercise	Facilitator leads discussion in the large group.	*(10 minutes)*
Exercise	**What situations make you physically tense?** Facilitator reminds participants of the home exercise they did the first week. In pairs, they choose and discuss three situations which are difficult for them (less or more than three is fine).	*(20 minutes)* *(10 minutes)*
	Feedback in large group.	*(10 minutes)*
Handout	**Relaxing in Everyday Situations** Facilitator distributes handout and goes through it, generating discussion.	*(20 minutes)*
Break	....	*(10 minutes)*
Exercise	**Walking with awareness** Participants go for a walk on their own, being aware of what muscles tense and relax. (Alternatively other situations could be used, such as making tea, using a machine or driving).	*(15 minutes)*
	Feedback	
Home exercise	**Differential relaxation in chosen situation** Choose one or all of the situations they have highlighted and undertake DR in it. (Those who want to can carry on	*(10 minutes)*

with a daily relaxation chosen from what they have learnt in
sessions 1 – 3.)

Exercise	**Relaxation**	*(20 minutes)*
	Facilitator leads PR and breathing relaxation.	
Closing circle	Something you are looking forward to.	*(10 minutes)*

4
HANDOUT

Relaxing in Everyday Situations

• • • The Problem

Many people are able to relax very well when stretched out on the floor listening to a relaxation tape. Unfortunately they are not able to put this into practice in everyday life. Soon after leaving the relaxation session, tension starts building up in their muscles and they are heading towards activation mode. Often the only reason for this is that living with tension has become a habit. It is only by releasing this everyday tension that an individual can truly become relaxed and learn the habit of relaxation.

There are two main ways in which this unwanted tension happens. One form involves putting far more effort into an action than is needed. Examples of this are gripping a pen so tightly that your hand goes white, or walking with heavy footsteps instead of lightly. The other involves using more muscles than are necessary to do a particular task. For instance, a person pushing a supermarket trolley may find they are tensing all the way up their arms, hunching their shoulders and tensing their backs. Often these two conditions occur together, making a really chronic tension problem.

• • • The Solution

To combat everyday tension, relaxation skills have to be taken from the relaxation session into everyday life, and used to work directly on individual areas of tension. There are three stages to this process.

1 Identifying the situations in which you are particularly prone to tension

These will be different according to the individual, but examples which often come up include driving, housework and repetitive tasks people have to do at work. Of course for many people tension can be apparent in whole areas of their life: how they sit and walk, for instance. In this case they need to apply these principles all the time.

2 *Identifying what unwanted tension is present in these situations*

Obviously some degree of tension is necessary for us to be able to function. Without it we would be blobs of jelly, and about as interesting. This stage involves finding out what muscles we need to tense, and how much, in order to do a task efficiently, and then being aware of how we are actually operating. Are we tensing parts of the body not necessary for this action?

3 *Releasing the unwanted tension*

The techniques we have already learnt can help with this stage. Progressive relaxation can be used on selected muscle groups. For experienced relaxers it may be enough to be aware of the muscle involved and release tension directly. Others may prefer to stretch and release the area. Breathing also can be brought into play, releasing tension on an out breath.

Part 4 **Differential Relaxation** **87**

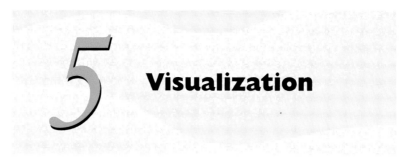

Visualization

• • • Objectives

By the end of the session participants will be able to:

- be aware of the mental and emotional effects of tension;
- understand the principles of mental relaxation;
- undertake a creative visualization independently.

Plan

Opening circle	Your dream holiday.	*(5 minutes)*
Feedback on home exercise	In the large group, participants feed back individually. Facilitator helps the group come up with solutions to any problems.	*(15 minutes)*
Handout	**Mental and Emotional Tension Checklist** Participants do the exercise individually. Feedback to group.	*(20 minutes)*
Handout	**Relaxing the Mind** Facilitator leads discussion on mental relaxation. Brief visualization exercise. Facilitator asks people to imagine the front of their house and gets feedback.	*(20 minutes)*
Break	....	*(10 minutes)*
Exercise	**Creative visualization 1** Facilitator does a couple of mini creative visualizations on different and contrasting themes, such as a beach walk or a crystal cave. Feedback	*(20 minutes)*
Exercise	**Creative visualization 2** Facilitator undertakes a relaxation exercise, starting with brief PR, then going on to visualization.	*(20 minutes)*

Feedback

Home exercise Participants choose a visualization to be part of their   *(5 minutes)*
relaxation sessions.

Closing circle Your favourite film.   *(5 minutes)*

5

Mental and Emotional Tension Checklist

HANDOUT

Mental and emotional tension can show itself in a number of ways. See how many of the following signs apply to you.

	Never	Occasionally	Often
Mental Tension			
Constant worry	❑	❑	❑
Feeling life is too demanding	❑	❑	❑
Feeling you can't cope	❑	❑	❑
Feeling inadequate	❑	❑	❑
Taking things too seriously	❑	❑	❑
Getting things out of perspective	❑	❑	❑
Feeling burdened	❑	❑	❑
Taking things personally	❑	❑	❑
Feeling frustrated	❑	❑	❑
Forgetfulness	❑	❑	❑
Problems in concentrating	❑	❑	❑
Problems in making decisions	❑	❑	❑
Worry when you've made decisions	❑	❑	❑
Obsessive thoughts	❑	❑	❑
Mind out of control	❑	❑	❑
Over-perfectionism	❑	❑	❑
Compulsions	❑	❑	❑

Others _____

Emotional Tension	Never	Occasionally	Often
Feeling irritable	❑	❑	❑
Feeling angry	❑	❑	❑
Mood swings	❑	❑	❑
Depression	❑	❑	❑
Withdrawal	❑	❑	❑
Feeling explosive	❑	❑	❑
Feeling trapped	❑	❑	❑
Feeling guilty	❑	❑	❑
Feeling hopeless	❑	❑	❑
Panic attacks	❑	❑	❑
Anxiety	❑	❑	❑
Feeling afraid	❑	❑	❑
Persistent relationship problems	❑	❑	❑
Abuse of alcohol, drugs, food	❑	❑	❑
Self-harm	❑	❑	❑

Others _____

Relaxing the Mind

5

HANDOUT

Often people find that, while learning to relax the body can be relatively simple, relaxing the mind is another story. Zen Buddhists talk about our 'Monkey Mind': the endless, nonsensical chatter which generally fills our mental space. Just as we are unconscious of physical tension, so we are often unaware how our minds go on (and on!). Take some time simply to observe what is going on in your head and you may be shocked at the second-rate soap opera that is playing.

More seriously many of us have a mental dialogue which is filled with negativity: compulsive thoughts, worries and fears can constantly fill our minds. These have an effect on our emotions — we feel fearful, anxious, inadequate — and on our bodies. Think about someone who is depressed. Do they stride out confidently or walk hesitantly, with rounded shoulders? Similarly angry or fearful thoughts can put us into activated stress mode.

While the body generally welcomes relaxation as a relief, the mind tends to cling tenaciously to its habitual thoughts. If we fight it, we create even more tension and our efforts are self-defeating. We need, then, a way of encouraging the mind to let go. One such method is visualization.

• • • Visualization

Visualization uses a function of the mind — the imagination — to calm the mind down. It is an extremely powerful tool, one which we use freely as a child but often neglect as we become older and more 'sensible'.

In visualization we use our imaginations to create scenes of beauty, peace, safety and calm. These scenes are interesting, so the nagging mind does not wish to interfere. Moreover, because of their nature, these scenes relax the body as well as the mind.

Visualization is based on imagined sensation: sight, hearing, taste, touch and smell. People experience these differently and with varying degrees of clarity, but everyone can visualize to the extent necessary for relaxation.

• • • A Short Example of Visualization

Perfect garden

You go down the steps and enter your perfect garden... your favourite flowers are in the beds ... you smell the scents ... and see the colours: blues, pinks, yellows ... the grass is green and lush under your bare feet ... you pass a waterfall which trickles over the rocks, bubbling and cascading ... the sound of the water relaxes you more and more ... you sit by the pool and listen to the sound ... above you the sky is blue, with white clouds ... birds sing and bees drone ... you are letting go completely.

• • • Use your Imagination

On the course a number of different relaxing scenes will be suggested to you, but most important is for you to use your own imagination to design visualizations which suit *you*.

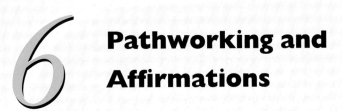

6 Pathworking and Affirmations

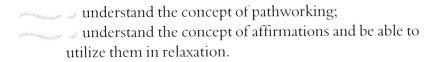

Objectives

By the end of the session participants will be able to:

- understand the concept of pathworking;
- understand the concept of affirmations and be able to utilize them in relaxation.

Plan

Opening circle

Something nice that has happened since last week. *(5 minutes)*

Feedback on home exercise

In the large group. *(10 minutes)*

Discussion

Evaluation of relaxation up to now *(15 minutes)*
Facilitator leads discussion on what effects relaxation has made on people's lives.

Handout

Pathworking and Affirmations *(10 minutes)*
Facilitator distributes handout and introduces the concept of pathworking.

Exercise

Pathworking *(20 minutes)*
Facilitator leads a pathworking relaxation.

Feedback

Break .... *(10 minutes)*

Exercise

Affirmations *(25 minutes)*
Facilitator introduces the concept of affirmations and gives a number of examples. Facilitator leads a relaxation exercise involving affirmations, such as PR followed by an affirmation, or a visualization involving affirmation.

Feedback

Home exercise Individuals choose an affirmation that is useful for them. *(15 minutes)*
There is discussion on how this can be incorporated into
their relaxation at home.

Closing circle A positive statement about yourself, such as "I am very *(10 minutes)*
kind", "I have beautiful eyes"
NB This exercise is often extremely difficult for some
people. The facilitator needs to be gently persistent.

Pathworking and Affirmations

• • • Pathworking

Pathworking is an advanced form of visualization in which the individual goes on a journey of the imagination. Pathworkings often involve making choices, meeting people, finding objects and so on. Sometimes they are guided visualizations, directed by a facilitator; alternatively they can be largely made up by the participants. Examples of pathworkings include:

Diving down to the bottom of the sea and finding treasure in a chest
Creating a safe place
Meeting your guardian angel — someone who loves you unconditionally

In relaxation, pathworking can be used to achieve a deep effect. It can also be a way of bringing relaxation into everyday life. For instance, the safe place can be returned to whenever you feel stressed. Similarly a pathworking could involve finding an object, such as a key, which is capable of relaxing you instantly.

• • • Affirmations

Affirmations are simple, positive statements which are used to programme the unconscious mind with positive messages, replacing the usual negative dialogue to which we subject ourselves. We are particularly receptive to affirmations when in a relaxed state, and in their turn affirmations can help us to relax even more deeply. They are always used in the present tense to make the sentiment more real.

Affirmations can be used throughout the relaxation session to deepen the experience. They can also be the focus of the session, being repeated a number of times at the end of a session in such a way that they will be imprinted on the unconscious mind and thus encourage us to be more relaxed in our everyday lives. The affirmations can be about general relaxation, or be specific, relating to actual events in which we want to be calm. Examples of affirmations include:

I am relaxing completely

I can relax at will

I am perfectly relaxed

When I go on stage I am completely relaxed

I am taking my driving test and I am perfectly calm

7 Meditation

Objectives

By the end of the session people will be able to:

 understand the key points of meditation;

practise a variety of meditation techniques.

Plan

Opening circle	The best present you have ever had.	*(10 minutes)*
Feedback on home exercise	In the large group.	*(15 minutes)*
Handout	**Meditation** Facilitator goes through handout, encouraging discussion.	*(25 minutes)*
Exercise	**Concentrating on the clock** Facilitator puts a clock with a prominent second hand in front of the group. They are to concentrate on this as long as they can. After a minute or so, the length they achieved is discussed.	*(5 minutes)*
Posture	Facilitator demonstrates and corrects posture.	*(10 minutes)*
Break	....	*(10 minutes)*
Exercise	**Visual meditation** Facilitator introduces a visual meditation exercise, for example, one using a flower, then leads it for about five minutes. Feedback	*(15 minutes)*
Exercise	**Mantra** Facilitator introduces a mantra exercise, such as 'Peace', then leads it for about five minutes. Feedback	*(15 minutes)*

Home exercise	Participants choose a form of meditation and practise it daily.	*(5 minutes)*
	Facilitator distributes Evaluating Relaxation Techniques handout and asks people to fill it in for next week.	
Closing circle	Something you are looking forward to.	*(5 minutes)*

7 Meditation

Meditation is an ancient method of stilling the mind to promote a feeling of peace and deep inner calm. To meditate you need to be able to sit still and quiet, and concentrate your mind on a repetitive word, thought or object.

While visualization calms the mind by the expansive use of imagination, meditation focuses the mind down so that it is concentrating on one thing. Thus unwanted thoughts are excluded from the mind by the object of concentration.

Meditation shares all the benefits of other relaxation techniques. However its effects are much further-reaching. The ultimate aim of meditation is a state of mind which is described as 'bliss' and a feeling of oneness with the universe. Most of us, perhaps, will have to settle for a sense of peace and calm and improved ability to cope with everyday life! One interesting state often associated with meditation is a feeling of space in the mind. Rather than our being overwhelmed by thoughts and ideas, meditation brings the ability to be detached and objective.

• • • Principles of Meditation

The first stage of meditation is to gain the ability to concentrate the mind. Physical posture is extremely important in meditation, which is always done in a seated position, with the back erect, stretched towards the ceiling. The head is slightly down. Eyes are shut or half open and focused on a point approximately three feet in front of you.

• • • Attitude of Mind

Although concentrating, the mind is not battling itself. As thoughts inevitably come into the mind, the trick is to allow them to come and go. Maintain awareness and let them pass through the mind without giving them attention. Allow them to die down through lack of interest. Thoughts are like clouds crossing the sky and disappearing, or like waves disappearing into ripples. Always bring your mind back to its object of meditation.

The mind is open, smiling, blossoming, relaxed, passive.

• • • Meditation Objects

Meditation objects can be:

visual — a flower, a painting, a candle;
a mantra — a word which is repeated out loud or in the
head, such as 'Peace', 'Love' or 'Om';
the breath — attention is focused on the breath (sometimes
breaths are counted);
visualizations — objects such as a river, colours or a
mountain are visualized in the mind.

Whatever the object, the technique is the same: gently but
persistently focus the mind.

Evaluating Relaxation Techniques

Score 0 – 10	Physically relaxing	Mentally relaxing	Enjoyable
Progressive relaxation			
Comments			

Breathing			
Comments			

Visualization			
Comments			

Pathworking			
Comments			

Affirmations			
Comments			

Meditation			
Comments			

Other			
Comments			

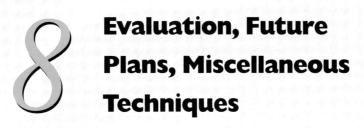

8 Evaluation, Future Plans, Miscellaneous Techniques

• • • Objectives

By the end of the session people will be able to:

- understand a variety of further relaxation methods;
- plan their future use of relaxation;
- evaluate their progress;
- evaluate the course.

Plan

Opening circle	If you could have any pet?	*(5 minutes)*
Feedback on home exercise	Discussion on meditation practice in the large group.	*(10 minutes)*
Exercise	**Evaluation of techniques** Facilitator leads discussion based on the evaluation handout in the large group.	*(10 minutes)*
Handout	**Other relaxation techniques** Facilitator distributes handout and leads discussion.	*(15 minutes)*
Exercise	**Relaxation tips** In small groups, participants list the things they do which they find relaxing, such as candle-lit baths. Facilitator writes suggestions on a flip chart in the big group.	*(20 minutes)*
Break		*(10 minutes)*
Discussion	**Future plans** Facilitator leads discussion on how people intend to incorporate relaxation into their lives in the future.	*(15 minutes)*
Handout	**Evaluation of Course** Forms are distributed and filled in.	*(10 minutes)*

| Exercise | **Final relaxation** | *(15 minutes)* |
| | Facilitator leads relaxation exercise of people's choice. | |

| Closing circle | A compliment to every member of the group from each member. | *(10 minutes)* |

Other Relaxation Techniques

HANDOUT

In addition to the techniques covered on this course there are a number of other activities which can be useful for relaxation. The more physical forms of relaxing can be especially suitable for people who find it hard to let go.

• • • Physical Exercise

Yoga
Yoga involves exercises which stretch and strengthen the body. The postures, or asanas, have been used for thousands of years and have a direct beneficial effect on the systems of the body. Most postures exercise the spine, the home of the central nervous system, through which messages are passed which control the whole body. Some yoga classes are dynamic, focusing on strong postures done very precisely. Others involve more gentle stretching, with an emphasis on relaxation. At the end of all yoga sessions there will be a relaxation based on some of the techniques discussed on this course.

Tai Chi
Rather than focusing on postures, tai chi is made up of a series of movements which combine into a form. The movements are both passive and active, and done in a way which involves awareness and control. The slow, precise movements of tai chi have a relaxing effect on the body and improve co-ordination and fitness.

Sports and exercise
Non-competitive sports and exercise can be relaxing. Many find swimming a good activity, as is walking and dancing. However relaxation is not a main aim of these forms of exercise, nor do they usually emphasize body awareness. Care must therefore be taken not to maintain unwanted tension while doing them.

The Alexander Technique
While not exactly a form of physical exercise, this technique teaches re-education of muscles and posture and can have a positive effect on stress-related problems.

• • • Massage

Many massage techniques will be extremely relaxing. The sense of giving control to another person while the muscles and joints are manipulated can promote a strong sense of well-being.

HANDOUT

Aromatherapy

Aromatherapy massage is especially effective, since the healing properties of essential oils are combined with physical stimulation. Aromatherapy massage can be done for the specific purpose of relaxation and stress reduction.

Reflexology

This is a precise form of massage using reflex points on the feet to stimulate the body's own healing potential. It does not diagnose or treat specific symptoms, but treats the whole person. It can have an extremely relaxing effect on the body.

• • • Miscellaneous

Flotation Tanks

Flotation tanks are purpose built tanks of salt water in which people float in darkness. Feedback indicates that they are extremely effective for relaxation.

Evaluation of Course

By completing the evaluation form you will help us to improve the next relaxation course. Please answer as fully as you can.

1 Has the relaxation course benefited you in any way? If so, how?

_____

_____

_____

2 Could the course have been improved in any way, for instance in terms of venue, facilitator, content or pace of course?

_____

_____

_____

3 Is there anything you would like to change about the relaxation course? For example, was anything not covered?

_____

_____

_____

4 Is there anything you found particularly helpful or enjoyable on the course?

_____

_____

_____

Thank you for your time.

Appendix

Stockists of Equipment

Snoezelen Equipment

Rompa
Freepost SF 10647
Goyt Side Rd
Chesterfield
Derbyshire
S40 2BR
United Kingdom

Flaghouse Inc
150 North MacQuesten Parkway
Mount Vernon
NY 10550
United States of America

Yoga Equipment

Mats and blocks (30 x 20 x 5cm)

Leisure Mats Ltd
Guide Bridge Mill
South Street
Ashton-under-Lyne
Manchester
OL7 0HU
United Kingdom

Hugger-Mugger Yoga Products
31 West Gregson Avenue
Salt Lake City
Utah 84115
United States of America

Yoga Mats
PO Box 885044
San Francisco
CA 94188
United States of America

Tools for Yoga
Rowland-Gallagher Inc
PO Box 99
Chatham
New Jersey 07928
United States of America

Relaxation Music

New World
Paradise Farm
Westhall
Halesworth
Suffolk
IP19 8RH
United Kingdom

Winslow
Telford Rd
Bicester
Oxon
OX6 0TS
United Kingdom

References

Bailey R, *Systematic Relaxation Tape*, Winslow, 1986.

Benson H, *The Relaxation Response*, Collins, 1975.

Davis M, Robbins Eshelman E & McKay M, *The Relaxation and Stress Reduction Workbook*, 3rd edn, New Harbinger Publications Inc, 5674 Shattuck Ave, Oakland, CA 94609, 1994.

Fontana D, *Managing Stress*, British Psychological Society and Routledge, 1989.

Gawain S, *Creative Visualisation*, New World Library, San Rafael, California, 1978.

Hewitt J, *The Complete Relaxation Book*, Rider, 1982.

Hewitt J, *Teach Yourself Meditation*, Hodder, 1984.

Holland S & Ward C, *Assertiveness: A Practical Approach*, Winslow, 1990.

Jacobson E, *You Must Relax*, Unwin, 1976.

Powell T, *The Mental Health Handbook*, Winslow, 1992.

Simmons M & Daw P, *Stress, Anxiety, Depression*, Winslow, 1994.

Tubbs I, *Creative Relaxation in Groupwork*, Winslow, 1996.

Williams G, *The Alexander Technique* (tape), VG Productions, 1991.

Also available from Winslow...

The Relaxation Therapy Manual

Christine Heron

This is a complete guide which enables those who already possess basic skills in therapeutic work with clients to use relaxation techniques with both individuals and groups. It is ideal for use by those with no background in relaxation as well as people with some experience who wish to refine their techniques.

Systematic Relaxation Tape

Roy Bailey

Anyone who uses relaxation as part of their treatment programme will welcome this invaluable pack which uses the Jacobsen approach. Suitable for use with individuals or groups, this audio-cassette tape is both versatile and flexible.

Creative Relaxation in Groupwork

Irene Tubbs

With more than 100 activities this unique text offers a goldmine of techniques and processes for relaxation. The text discusses the benefits of relaxation, covers theoretical and practical relaxation methods, provides constructive guidelines and incorporates actual workshop themes.

Creative Games in Groupwork

Robin Dynes

Presented in a format that immediately allows you to see what materials are needed, how much preparation is required and how each game is played, this book will be of real practical value to the user.

Creative Action Methods in Groupwork

Andy Hickson

Highly practical and accessible, with emphasis on participative groupwork and good working practices, this unique manual outlines action method techniques for exploring difficulties and problems.

Creative Writing in Groupwork

Robin Dynes

Here are more than 100 stimulating activities designed to help participants express themselves, explore situations, compare ideas and develop both imagination and creative ability.

Creative Drama in Groupwork

Sue Jennings

150 ideas for drama in this completely practical manual make it a veritable treasure trove which will inspire everyone to run drama sessions creatively, enjoyably and effectively.

Creative Movement & Dance in Groupwork

Helen Payne

This innovative book explores the link between movement and emotion and provides 180 activities and ideas with a clear rationale for the use of dance movement to enrich therapy programmes.

Creative Art in Groupwork

Jean Campbell

Highly accessible, this manual contains 142 art activities developed specifically for use with groups of people of all ages.

For further information or to obtain a free copy of the Winslow catalogue, please contact:

WINSLOW

Telford Road • Bicester
Oxon OX6 0TS • UK
Tel: (01869) 244644
Fax: (01869) 320040